THE PHARAOHS

TREASURES OF THE WORLD

THE PHARAOHS

by

Lionel Casson

STONEHENGE

Treasures of the World was created and
produced by

TREE COMMUNICATIONS, INC.

PRESIDENT
Rodney Friedman

PUBLISHER
Bruce Michel

VICE PRESIDENTS
Ronald Gross
Paul Levin

EDITOR
Charles L. Mee, Jr.

EXECUTIVE EDITOR
Shirley Tomkievicz

ART DIRECTOR
Sara Burris

PICTURE EDITOR
Mary Zuazua Jenkins

ASSOCIATE EDITORS
Thomas Dickey   Vance Muse   Henry Wiencek

ASSISTANT ART DIRECTOR
Carole Muller

ASSISTANT PICTURE EDITORS
Carol Gaskin   Charlie Holland

COPY EDITOR
Lilyan Glusker

ASSISTANT COPY EDITOR
Fredrica A. Harvey

EDITORIAL ASSISTANTS
Martha J. Brown   Janet Sullivan

FOREIGN RESEARCHERS
Rosemary Klein Burgis (London)
Mirka Gondicas (Athens)
Alice Jugie (Paris)
Dee Pattee (Munich)
Simonetta Toraldo (Rome)

CONSULTING EDITORS
Joseph J. Thorndike, Jr.
Dr. Ulrich Hiesinger

The series is published under the supervision of

STONEHENGE PRESS INC.

PUBLISHER
John Canova

EDITOR
Ezra Bowen

DEPUTY EDITOR
Carolyn Tasker

THE AUTHOR: Lionel Casson is Andrew W. Mellon Professor of Classical Studies at the American Academy in Rome, as well as professor of classics at New York University. He is the author of *Ancient Egypt* in Time-Life's *Great Ages of Man*, among other books, and of articles on Greek, Roman, and Egyptian history for *Horizon* magazine.

CONSULTANT FOR THIS BOOK: Robert Steven Bianchi is the associate curator in the Department of Egyptian and Classical Art at The Brooklyn Museum. A well-known author and lecturer, Dr. Bianchi has taught Egyptian art for CBS-TV on *Sunrise Semester* and on the graduate level at Columbia University.

COVER: *The falcon god of ancient Egypt spreads its wings under a red sun. Tutankhamen owned this pendant of gold and inlaid stones.*

TITLE PAGE: *The Great Sphinx at Giza lies before Khafre's pyramid. Both monuments were built during the twenty-sixth century* B.C.

OVERLEAF: *Two noblemen go fowling, a favorite sport of Egyptian nobility, in this fifteenth-century-*B.C. *tomb painting.*

ABOVE: *Amen, the supreme god of Egypt, holds a scimitar and the Key of Life. The gold statuette is from Karnak's Great Temple.*

CONTENTS

I EGYPT'S FIRST PHARAOHS 10
picture essay: The Tomb Touching Heaven 16
portfolio: The Vanity of Princesses 25

II THE LIFE OF LUXURY 40
portfolio: The Imperial High Life 49

III THE ECCENTRIC ROYAL COUPLE 66
picture essay: Beauty in the Round 72
portfolio: The Radical's Splendid City 81

IV THE GOLDEN BOY-KING 96
portfolio: A Boy-King's Golden Trove 105

V A LEGACY OF RUINS 140
picture essay: Homage to a Beautiful Companion 146
portfolio: A Massive Stone Legacy 155

Maps 8
Chronology 170
Acknowledgments & Credits 172
Suggested Readings 173
Index 173

The ancient Egyptian world was, as it is today,
defined by the great Nile, opposite. Since the river
flows northward, emptying into the Mediterranean,
the area nearer its source is called Upper Egypt.
The rich delta region is Lower Egypt. Major cities,
mines, and monuments are indicated on the map,
as are five cataracts within the river—veins of granite that cut across the riverbed forming broken,
rock-studded rapids. Pyramid sites are marked by
triangles. The map below is a large picture of the
ancient Egyptians' neighbors.

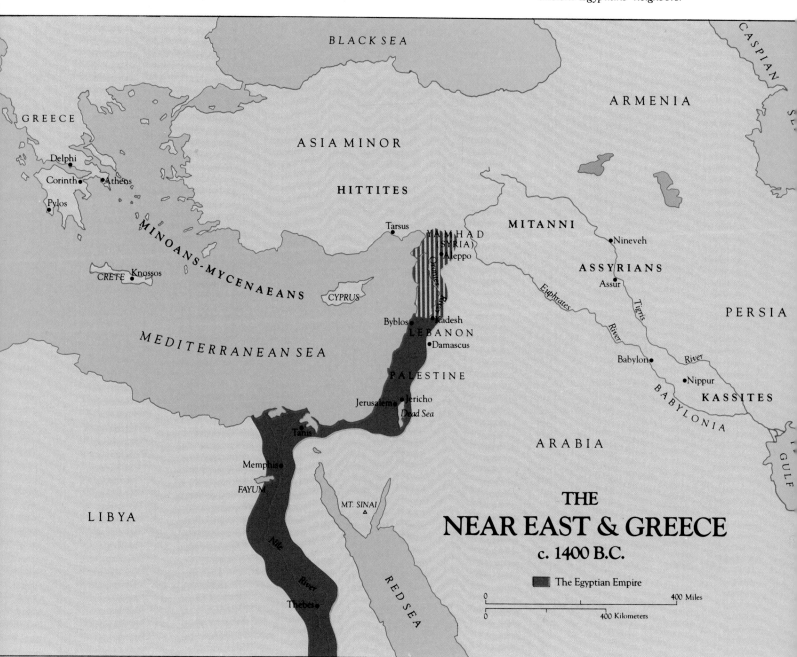

THE
NEAR EAST & GREECE
c. 1400 B.C.

The Egyptian Empire

0 ————————— 400 Miles

0 ————————— 400 Kilometers

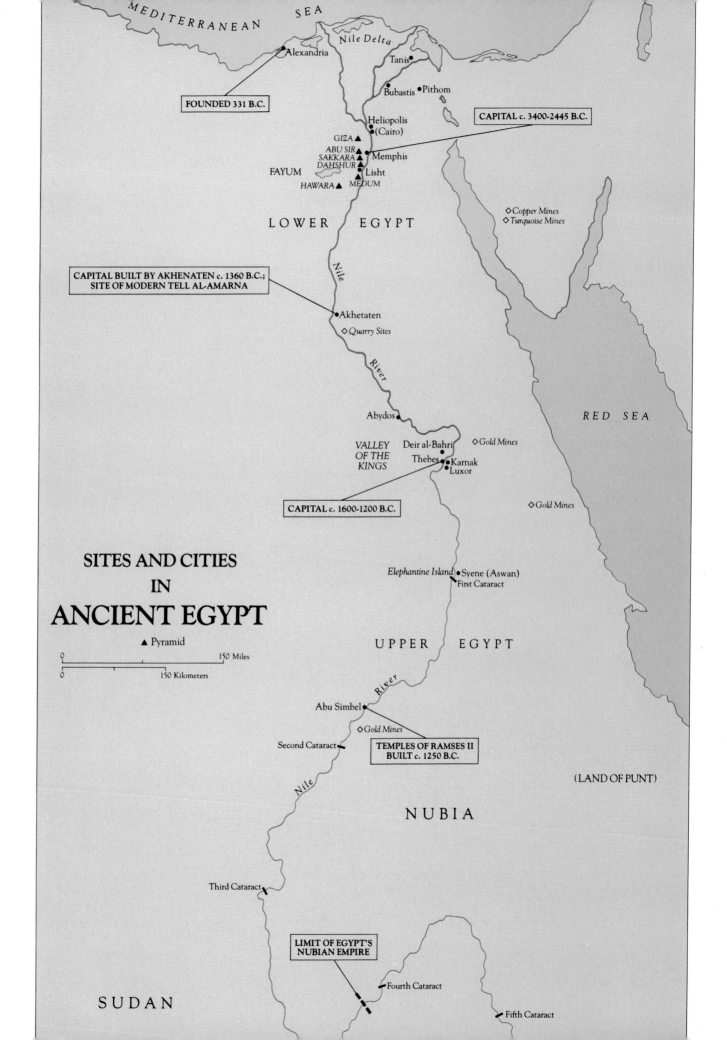

MEDITERRANEAN SEA

Nile Delta

Alexandria

FOUNDED 331 B.C.

Tanis

Bubastis • Pithom

Heliopolis
(Cairo)

CAPITAL c. 3400-2445 B.C.

GIZA ▲
ABU SIR ▲
SAKKARA ▲
DAHSHUR ▲ Memphis

FAYUM   ▲ Lisht

HAWARA ▲ ▲ MEDUM

LOWER   EGYPT

◇*Copper Mines*
◇*Turquoise Mines*

Nile

**CAPITAL BUILT BY AKHENATEN c. 1360 B.C.;
SITE OF MODERN TELL AL-AMARNA**

• Akhetaten

◇*Quarry Sites*

River

RED   SEA

Abydos •

◇*Gold Mines*

*VALLEY
OF THE
KINGS*

Deir al-Bahri •
Thebes • • Karnak
• Luxor

CAPITAL c. 1600-1200 B.C.

◇*Gold Mines*

SITES AND CITIES
IN
ANCIENT EGYPT

▲ Pyramid

0 _____ 150 Miles
0 _____ 150 Kilometers

Elephantine Island • Syene (Aswan)
First Cataract

UPPER   EGYPT

River

Abu Simbel •

◇*Gold Mines*

Second Cataract

**TEMPLES OF RAMSES II
BUILT c. 1250 B.C.**

(LAND OF PUNT)

Nile

NUBIA

Third Cataract

**LIMIT OF EGYPT'S
NUBIAN EMPIRE**

• Fourth Cataract

SUDAN

• Fifth Cataract

I

EGYPT'S FIRST PHARAOHS

AND THE GIFT OF THE NILE

In the land of Egypt there lived a unique people with a very special attitude toward treasure. Egyptians—at least those who could afford it—were concerned all their lives with accumulating and hoarding precious objects to store away in their tombs, particularly objects of gold, a metal which occurred in rich deposits and was mined from very early times on. As a consequence, Egypt provides not only the earliest treasures in the world but continues to provide them in all periods of her history. When excavators began poking about in her ruins, treasure came trickling out of her tombs, at times, as in the case of Tutankhamen, pouring out.

The treasure survived, thanks to yet another special feature of Egypt: the climate. Some rain falls on the delta of the Nile, but south of that point it gets ever scarcer. In Upper Egypt—the south—there is hardly any. The earth, perennially dry, can preserve perfectly for millennia whatever is laid away or abandoned in it, from mummified bodies to fragile papyrus or textiles.

About 2650 B.C., King Djoser built the first colossal Egyptian pyramid. This stone statue from its base is the oldest portrait of a pharaoh.

Egypt, as a result, is a storehouse of antiquities.

Act One of Egyptian history opens with the creation, about 3000 B.C., of the first unified state in history. Before this, however, there was an extended prelude during which her primitive population gradually came to understand how to exploit the remarkable river on whose banks it lived.

"Egypt is the gift of the Nile," wrote the Greek historian Herodotus. He made the observation after a visit about the middle of the fifth century B.C.; the Egyptians had become aware of the fact at least thirty centuries earlier. They inhabited a ribbon of lush, green land that slashed through a vast stretch of sterile desert, an elongated oasis as it were, formed by the path of the river. The Nile's sources lie in the highlands far to the south. Every year between July and November its waters, swollen by tropical rains and loaded with silt, spilled out of their bed as they swept through Egypt to the sea, flooding far and wide on both sides. Upon receding, they left behind a layer of fertile mud made up of the silt they had been carrying. All people had to do was plant in it and tend. There was no need to manure, rotate crops, let fields lie fallow.

This irrigation and enrichment that nature provided was a boon indeed. But its value could be made even greater by human collaboration—by farmers joining forces to dig catch basins for trapping water and storing it for the dry months, to dig and maintain canals leading to these basins and from them to the fields, to share out equally during the dry months the water that was hoarded. And the value increased still more if the collaboration took place not just here and there but throughout the entire length of the Nile. Thus there came into being within the populace a pressure to form bigger political units, a pressure that culminated in a unified nation. Only a unified nation could coordinate work all along the Nile to its very mouth.

This epoch-making event happened shortly before 3000 B.C., when a certain leader named Menes, starting from Upper Egypt fought his way north and conquered to the shores of the

Spears at the ready, boatmen cruise the Nile in search of hippopotamuses for a kilted dignitary named Ti, who towers above them. The painted stone relief is from Ti's Old Kingdom tomb at Sakkara.

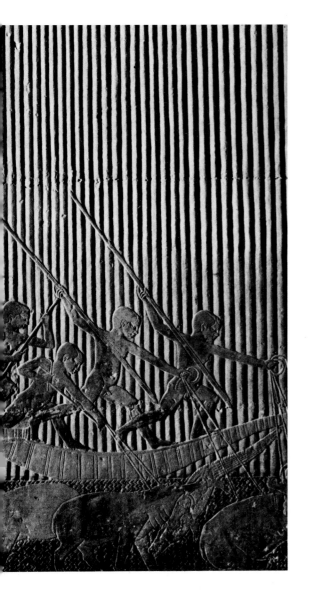

Mediterranean. We know no more about him than that. He may even be a figure of legend rather than fact. Legendary or not, the Egyptians honored him as the first king to rule over the whole valley of the Nile, and historians as the founder of the so-called First Dynasty. Manetho, an Egyptian priest who lived about 300 B.C., conceived the idea of dividing up Egypt's long history into thirty dynasties, each embracing the years when members of the same family held the throne; the idea proved so useful that historians have followed it to this day. The last dynasty, the Thirty-first, marked the sad moment, some two-and-a-half millennia after Menes' achievement, when Egypt fell to Alexander the Great and ceased to exist as an independent nation.

The Egyptians gave Menes the title of pharaoh. The word literally means "great house"; originally it must have referred to the palace where he lived and then was transferred to the occupant. Menes' successors chose as the site for their "great house" the city of Memphis in Lower Egypt.

Under these successors the Nile poured out those blessings that made Egypt far and away the richest nation of antiquity. She flourished not only in plenty but in peace. For she enjoyed yet another geographical boon—relatively secure natural boundaries. To the north was the Mediterranean and on the other three sides, desert. Nor could an enemy attack by floating down the Nile, because five cataracts—waterfalls—barred the way, from the Fifth, deep in the Sudan, to the First, at Syene (today called Aswan), the southern limit of the pharaohs' realm.

Egypt prospered so, that by 2700 B.C. she had entered upon her first great age, the one historians call the Old Kingdom (2700–2200 B.C.). This was when the celebrated pyramids were built. The first, for Pharaoh Djoser, rose in a series of steps, a design that derived naturally from the traditional mounds the Egyptians put over their graves. As Egypt's power and wealth grew, so did its pyramids: Djoser's was soon followed by the Great Pyramids, the trio of true pyramids at Giza just outside Cairo that housed the remains of Khufu, Khafre, and Menkaure—or

In this frieze from a tomb at Sakkara, workers in marshes along the Nile carry bundles of papyrus reeds to be made into paper.

Cheops, Chefren, and Mycerinus, as Herodotus called them, doing his best to transliterate the unfamiliar names into Greek—those members of the mighty Fourth Dynasty who ruled from roughly 2600 to 2500 B.C. The Great Sphinx at Giza, with the body of a lion and the face of the pharaoh Khafre, is another masterwork of this halcyon century. Fed by the Nile and protected by the deserts, Egypt paid scant attention to the important neighbors rising about her, the Sumerians and Akkadians in Mesopotamia or the Canaanites along the Levant.

And her own way meant a very special culture and society, in which the key figure, towering over all, was the pharaoh. He dominated his land and people as no ruler has ever done since, for he was not only a king but a god incarnate. By divine right he enjoyed the exploitation of all his subjects' skills and muscle and the ownership of every grain of his country's soil. During his lifetime he dwelt in the "great house" in august splendor amid his many wives, one of whom, almost always of royal blood, he would raise above the others and acknowledge as queen. After his death he was laid to rest in a tomb worthy of a god.

The Great Pyramids, which must have demanded an immense expenditure of the nation's resources, were not built, as people tend to think, by forced labor, by whiplashed slaves, or foreign captives. Egypt never went in much for slavery, either at this time or later, and at this time it certainly did not get involved in any major foreign wars. Work on the pyramids was carried out by the pharaoh's devoted subjects; it was their contribution to the sacred being whose beneficence, they were convinced, was responsible for their well-being. The Nile, that most accommodating of rivers, behaved in such a way as to render this contribution no hardship. When the river was in flood, work on the fields was out of the question, for they were underwater. Thus Egypt's peasantry was available for rounding up into gangs for quarrying and hauling stone; indeed, they must have welcomed being fed at the pharaoh's expense.

God though he was, the pharaoh could not run the state all by himself. So there gradually came into existence a court of nobles to assist him, with whom he shared some of his bounty. He assigned them land for their own use and peasants to work it for them. He allowed them the most precious of privileges, the right to erect their tombs close to his, close to the holy resting place of his divine bones.

Though critically important, the pharaoh was far from being the Egyptians' only divinity. They also worshiped the sun, the moon, and a host of other gods that were unusual combinations of humans and animals. Then there was their attitude toward the hereafter. They conceived of the next world as an endless continuation of life on earth—only better, since it could be counted on to be consistently happy. Thus, in their thinking, the manner of burial was of paramount importance; after all, it would determine how one was to abide for eternity.

First the body had to be rendered impervious to decay. This was effected through mummification, the drying out of a cadaver by packing it for a while in natron (a form of sodium carbonate common in Egypt), and, when it was dry, anointing it with oils and resins and aromatics and swathing it in linen bandages. A tomb had to be prepared that was in the form of a complete dwelling and stocked with everything one had used on earth and would presumably need in the afterlife. For a poor peasant, burial meant a corpse hastily and carelessly mummified and stacked in a common grave. For a noble it meant a corpse that was mummified with exquisite care (the viscera removed and the cavities packed with resins and aromatics), wrapped in the finest of garments, decked with precious jewelry, and laid away in a tomb that was a replica of a mansion and was filled with superb furniture and the full range of household objects.

For a pharaoh burial meant even more. Cheops, for example, received the greatest tomb monument ever built, a pyramid that took hordes of workmen over two decades to complete. In two long pits nearby were placed—knocked down, to be sure, but all the parts were there—two noble Nile boats to carry the sacred

Two men fill baskets with figs while hungry baboons compete with them for the fruit. This scene is from the wall of a tomb sealed in about 1890 B.C.

TEXT CONTINUED ON PAGE 20

THE TOMB TOUCHING HEAVEN

When Cheops died about 2556 B.C., his body—probably borne along the Nile on a funerary boat (see overleaf)—was brought to a necropolis that astonishes mankind to this day. The Great Pyramid at Giza, right, built during the pharaoh's twenty-three-year reign, was the center of a vast complex of mortuary temples, statues, monuments, and lesser tombs of the pharaoh's family. The pyramid itself, originally finished with a sheath of white limestone and capped with gold, covers thirteen acres and rises to a height of nearly five hundred feet.

The massive project was a labor of piety for the pharaoh's thousands of devoted subjects who quarried six million tons of stone, transported the individual blocks (most weighing at least six thousand pounds each), and somehow raised them into place. Though they used only simple arithmetic, the pyramid builders were able to calculate nearly perfect geometric forms, and Cheops' tomb may have had some astronomical function: its corners are oriented to the four points of the compass. Within the Great Pyramid are passageways and galleries, as well as the magnificent chamber in its heart where the pharaoh's mummy was placed—and from which it vanished—long ago.

Beyond the ruins of the satellite tombs of the pharaoh's family, Cheops' Great Pyramid rises toward the sky. An ancient Egyptian hymn likens the ascent of the pharaoh's spirit from the pyramid to the rush of a heron and the leap of a grasshopper.

Recovered from a pit near the Great Pyramid, the royal boat of Cheops—the world's oldest surviving yacht—may have last seen service as the king's funerary barge. An impressive length (140 feet) and made of fine cedar, the boat nonetheless simulated a humble raft of papyrus—which in Egyptian mythology carried the sun god to heaven. The shipwrights knew their craft well, carving palm and papyrus motifs throughout the boat, and devising intricate sliding locks for the doors. Though its individual planks were sewn together with rope, the vessel is watertight. On pleasure cruises on the Nile during his life, the king probably sat in the front pavilion as his servants manned the oars.

TEXT CONTINUED FROM PAGE 15

body in state on its last passage to the afterworld.

This concentration on death and what lay beyond did not derive from a gloomy morbidity, was not the expression of a ghost-haunted people. On the contrary, it came from serene, confident conviction. The Egyptians were a gay, cocky race. This is apparent in the pictures they put on the walls of their tombs, scenes from daily life that the deceased would be reliving in the hereafter. These are full of cheer and humor: children romping in play while the grown-ups work in the fields, two girls in a hair-pulling fight while their companions busily harvest, the transport of grain coming to a halt when a donkey in the line plants his feet and refuses to budge, comic consternation in a carpentry shop when the foreman unexpectedly drops in.

The Egyptians made their elaborate preparations for the hereafter with joyous anticipation: things are fine now, but they will be even better then. There may have been an element of calculation behind this. Life expectancy was short in those days, some thirty years at the most, so whatever happened on earth was inevitably fleeting; it was far more rewarding to concentrate on a boundless happiness after death. They were confident, as they were of so much else, that they would remain in their tombs undisturbed to bask in this happiness for eternity. Eternity proved to be, in some cases, less than a few generations.

A servant crouches to wash and polish a food jar. The painted limestone tomb figure assured its owner that he would have the servant's loyalty, and abundant provisions, throughout eternity.

Hard times came even to the blessed land of Egypt and brought to an end the golden years of the Old Kingdom. Deserts are useful boundaries, but determined attackers can cross them, and groups of these eventually began to cause trouble in the Sinai to the northeast. The pharaohs were hampered by the lack of a good army. Peaceful Egypt's manpower had been trained to build pyramids and temples, not to carry arms. To make matters worse, the nobles of the court started jockeying for power.

Had there been a strong hand on the helm, crisis might have been averted. But, shortly after 2300 B.C., a child pharaoh,

Pepi II, inherited the throne and reigned for ninety years. His last years, as one might expect, were feeble. Powerful nobles broke away, and, soon after his death, civil war engulfed the land. Lawlessness was widespread. Egypt's tombs, enticingly full of treasure and now unguarded, were easy prey for robbers. "This land is helter-skelter," wailed a writer of the age. "I show thee the son as a foe, the brother as an enemy, and a man killing his own father ... I show thee the land topsy-turvy."

Topsy-turvy it was indeed: for eight hundred years a god-king had reigned from the capital, and now he had been deposed from his sanctified seat by mere mortals. Things remained in this state until finally, about 2000 B.C., a new and strong dynasty took hold and ushered in the second key period of Egyptian history, the one historians call the Middle Kingdom.

It lasted roughly from 2000 to 1800 B.C., during which time half a dozen pharaohs—three named Amenemhet and three Senusret—energetic and conscientious rulers, restored the country's political health. They came originally from the south of Egypt, and it was nearer there that they set their capital, in the stretch of desert now called the Fayum, not far from the modern town of Lisht. One of the great benefits they bestowed upon the area was the building of a vast catch basin which provided water enough to carve twenty-seven thousand acres out of the desert and convert it to farmland.

They ended once and for all Egypt's isolation. The facts had to be faced: during the years of unrest, marauders had plagued the borders, particularly the southern border at the First Cataract. The Middle Kingdom pharaohs sent soldiers there, annexed territory as far as the Second Cataract, and extended Egyptian influence as deep as the Third. This brought a bonanza in its wake: the gold mines of Nubia. Gold was not scarce in Egypt proper; there were rich deposits in the south, in the desert between the Nile and the Red Sea. But Nubia had richer ones, in the valley from the Second to the Third Cataract.

To the northeast the pharaohs contented themselves with

A woman carries a live duck and a basket of meats, offerings for a Thebes chancellor, in whose tomb she was buried about 2050 B.C. The wooden tomb model stands nearly four feet tall.

fortifying the border, although they were willing to mount an occasional raid beyond. They preferred to send merchants rather than soldiers, to encourage commerce between Egypt and the Levant and even farther. Caravans moved freely back and forth.

The pharaohs of the Middle Kingdom commanded the wealth and manpower to mark their graves with pyramids, though far more modest ones than the soaring structures of their Old Kingdom predecessors. Inside the tombs, however, was treasure just as precious, some of which escaped the hands of tomb robbers and fell into those of archaeologists. Just before the end of the last century, a French excavator, Jacques de Morgan, made a lucky strike: at Dahshur, where Senusret III was buried, he found the jewelry of six of the king's daughters.

But this was eclipsed by the find made by Britain's famed Egyptologist Sir Flinders Petrie not long after. While working in the area of the pyramid of Senusret II in 1914, he hit a treasure trove in the grave of one of the king's daughters, Sit-Hathor-Yunet. Ancient robbers had been there before him and had stripped the mummy; but, in a hurry and with only dim light, they had overlooked the princess' jewel boxes. The break-in unsealed the tomb; for centuries the desert sands poured in and so did the annual overflow of the Nile. When Petrie's men entered, they found the contents scattered all about and embedded in a mass of dried mud. They had to pick at it painfully with penknife and pin to extract the tiny bits of jewelry without doing damage. It was well worth the effort; from the dirt and dust was resurrected a dazzling display: the princess' wig ornaments, crown, necklace, anklets, bracelets, pectorals.

Middle Kingdom treasure shows prodigal use of gold; this is what we would expect, now that the pharaohs had at their disposal the mines of Nubia. It shows, as well, prodigal use of what we would consider merely semiprecious stones—carnelian, turquoise, and lapis lazuli. The Egyptians themselves may have considered carnelian semiprecious, since it was locally available, but probably not the turquoise and certainly not the lapis.

Gathered beneath the wings of the falcon king, a bee, plant, cobra, and vulture—various symbols of Egypt—submit to the pharaoh's rule. These hieroglyphs are raised in gold on the columns of Queen Hetepheres' canopy at right.

Cheops' mother, Hetepheres, dwelled and slept in luxury in this gilded bedroom, furnished for her by her husband, King Snefru. The slender box of inlaid veneers and gold was a storage chest for linen curtains, which hung over the columns of the canopy to screen out insects and also to ensure the queen's privacy.

THE ROYAL BEDCHAMBER

Cabinetmakers of Egypt's Old Kingdom used the metal tools developed by their prehistoric ancestors to make elegant furniture from Lebanese cedar, Syrian conifers, ebony, and other fine woods. The hot climate of Egypt called for austere, airy interiors, such as the bedroom, above, of Queen Hetepheres. The bed, chair, box, and canopy—all of gilded wood—were recovered from the queen's tomb near her son Cheops' Great Pyramid. The queen's bed was designed according to the preference of the Egyptian aristocracy for sleeping on a slant: the headrest is higher than the footboard. The mattresses were cushioned with layers of sheets. Wealthy Egyptians took great pride in their beds, which distinguished them from the poor, who slept on the ground.

The daughters of a prince of the Middle Kingdom, Djehutyhotep, hold fragrant blue lotus flowers in this relief of painted limestone from their father's tomb at Deir al-Bersha.

Turquoise came from the Sinai desert, and lapis all the way from the abundant deposits at Badakhshan in the northeastern corner of Afghanistan. The lines of trade reached far.

These lines of trade put another metal into the hands of Egypt's craftsmen—silver, which was not to be found in their own country. In tombs of the Old Kingdom, when Egypt lived in isolation, silver objects are rare. In the Middle Kingdom, they become increasingly common. The metal was mined in Anatolia and Armenia; understandably it was more valuable in Egyptian eyes than gold. Archaeologists have found at one Middle Kingdom site a batch of no less than 153 silver cups. They were a gift to Amenemhet II from some kinglet in the Levant, perhaps one of the rulers of the Phoenician port of Byblos.

When the third Senusret died, shortly after 1850 B.C., the dynasty's strength began to weaken. The next 150 years saw a succession of ineffectual pharaohs. And then, about 1675 B.C., Egypt suffered a disaster, something that had never happened to her during thirteen centuries as a nation: foreign invasion.

The Egyptians called their attackers the Hyksos, a vague name that means "rulers of the foreign lands." They seem to have been, at least at the outset, leaders of nomadic bands. As time passed, there was a steady increase in their size and strength. What is more, they possessed the up-to-date weaponry that had been developed in Asia, far superior to the equipment of Egyptian soldiers. These had only a feeble type of bow and arrow and wore no body armor; the fighting men of the Hyksos wore armor, wielded a bow that shot an arrow with destructive force, and, to top it all, their leaders rode into battle in horse-drawn chariots. Hyksos bands swept easily over the northeastern frontier, set up a capital in the delta, brought all the land up to Thebes under their direct rule, and made Thebes itself a vassal state.

The Hyksos were hated, despised foreigners. The Egyptians waited for the moment when they would garner the strength to turn them out. It came soon enough—and marked the beginning of the country's next great period, the New Kingdom.

THE VANITY OF PRINCESSES

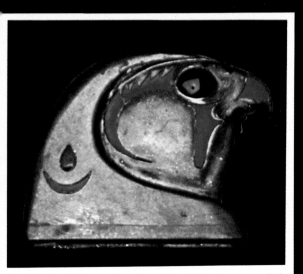

A dark-eyed falcon, from the collar of a princess, symbolizes Horus, ancient Egypt's watchful god. Only those the pharaoh favored could wear such elaborate jewelry.

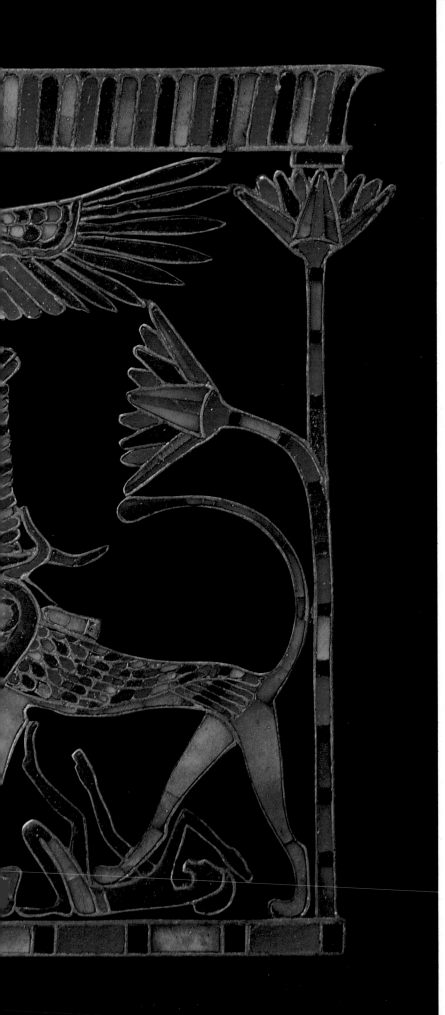

In the royal house of King Senusret III were three princesses—Mereret, Khnumet, and Sit-Hathor-Yunet—whose fabulous jewelry, here and on the following pages, was typical of the Middle Kingdom. The princesses must have loved their jewelry, most of which was given to them by the pharaoh. Intending to be properly bespangled in the afterlife, they took it with them to their tombs. The ancient Egyptians appreciated the allure of jewelry, and both men and women wore it not only to enhance their appearance but also to display their wealth and to guard against evil and danger. The most valued jewelry was of gold, inlaid with carnelian, turquoise, and lapis lazuli, which were preferred for their natural colors: blood red, the green of springtime, and the blue of sky and water. Egyptian jewelers created delicate necklaces, crowns, bracelets, rings, and pendants, decorating them with plants and animals and hieroglyphic symbols. By filling cellular networks of pure gold with cut stones, the Egyptians perfected a kind of cloisonné for larger pectorals and collars.

Jewelers enjoyed high social status and handsome rewards, but their lives were never easy or glamorous: many lost their eyesight in the excruciatingly detailed work, as they labored with primitive tools over the awful heat of charcoal braziers. Their craft was a family enterprise, with fathers training sons to master the basic techniques in childhood, so that they might spend as many years as possible producing precious treasures for rich and powerful patrons.

Within a shrine supported by columns of lotus flowers, King Senusret III—represented by a pair of falcon-headed sphinxes—tramples and subjugates Egypt's enemies. The vulture goddess oversees the event. This pectoral of Princess Mereret consists of an outline of gold cells filled with precious stones.

Using plant and animal designs and hieroglyphic symbols, Middle Kingdom jewelers created this exquisite jewelry for Princess Mereret. The pendant at left bears a lotus design, and golden cowrie shells form the girdle beneath it. The necklace at right, of precious stones and gold beads, is hung with hieroglyphs standing for "all protection in life." Golden lions lie within the chains of the two bracelets.

LOTUS PENDANT

GIRDLE OF GOLDEN SHELLS

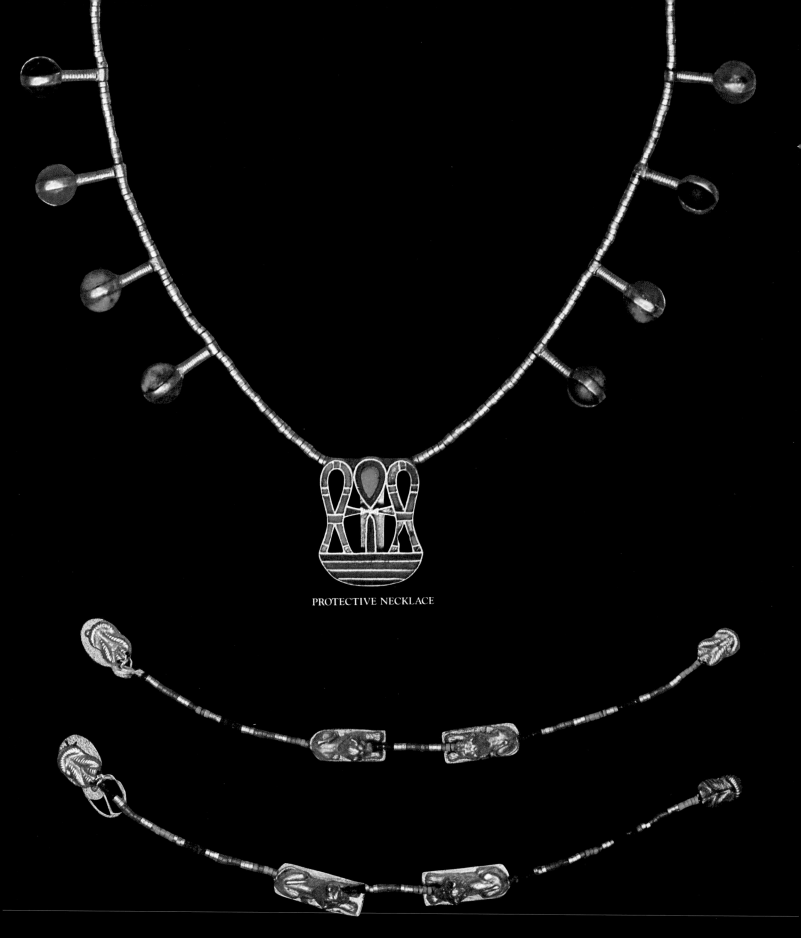

PROTECTIVE NECKLACE

LION BRACELETS

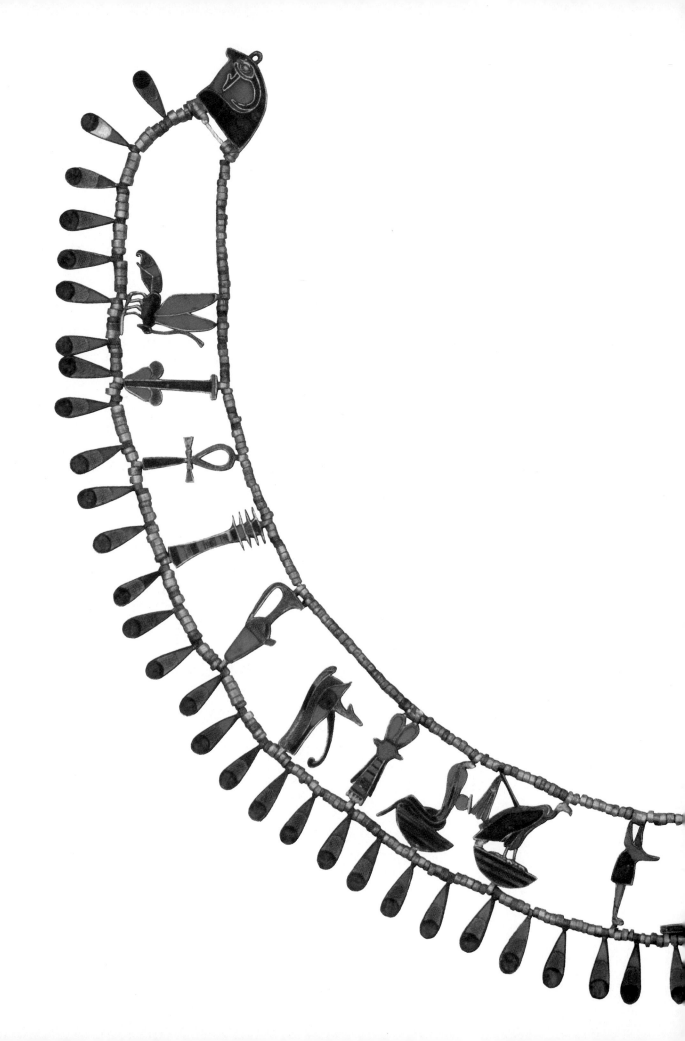

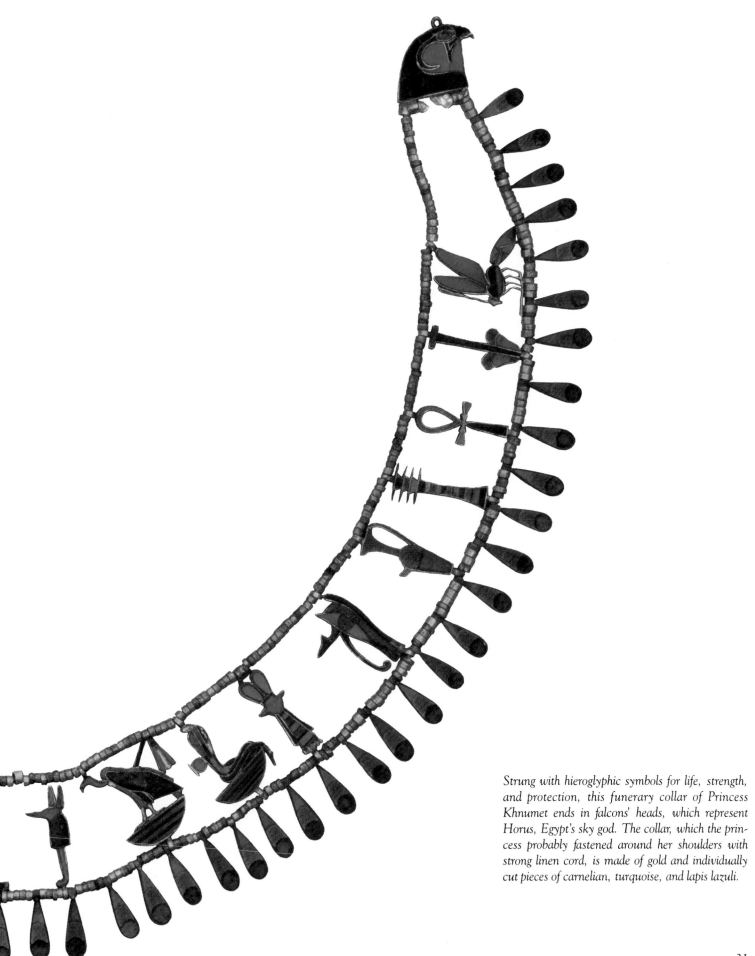

Strung with hieroglyphic symbols for life, strength, and protection, this funerary collar of Princess Khnumet ends in falcons' heads, which represent Horus, Egypt's sky god. The collar, which the princess probably fastened around her shoulders with strong linen cord, is made of gold and individually cut pieces of carnelian, turquoise, and lapis lazuli.

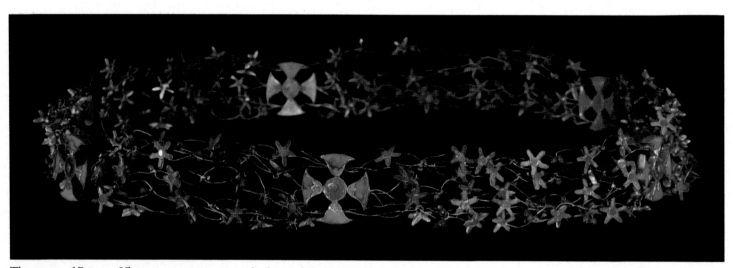

The crown of Princess Khnumet comprises a wreath of twisted flowering vines made of tiny cloisonné flowers threaded on fine gold wires.

Ribbons of solid gold hang from Sit-Hathor-Yunet's crown, which is topped by the pharaonic cobra and a plume that quivered and flashed as the princess moved about. Cloisonné rosettes add an element of delicate natural beauty to the crown, a symbol of power and authority.

On her hips and sandaled feet, Sit-Hathor-Yunet wore purple and gold jewelry, such as the belt and anklets here. Leopards' heads of gold alternate with double strands of amethyst beads on the belt, and a golden cat's claw is attached to each anklet.

The Egyptians used cosmetics against the parching sun and wind—as well as for good looks. The most privileged kept their toiletries in lovely chests, such as this one of ivory-inlaid ebony, which belonged to Sit-Hathor-Yunet. Scattered about are its contents: a silver mirror, two copper and gold razors, whetstones, and various jars for rouge and ointments.

A figure kneeling between two enormous falcon gods symbolizes eternity in this pectoral, a gift from King Senusret II to his daughter, Sit-Hathor-Yunet. Nearly four hundred pieces of precious colored stones went into the pectoral, which hung from a necklace of gold, carnelian, green feldspar, and lapis lazuli.

II

THE LIFE OF LUXURY

IN THE DAYS OF EMPIRE

No man can settle down, when despoiled by the taxes of
the Asiatics. I will grapple with him, that I may rip open
his belly! My wish is to save Egypt and to smite the
Asiatics!" So wrote Kamose, the ruler of Thebes, smarting under
the allegiance he was forced to pledge to the Hyksos overlords.
The moment came when he felt confident enough to revolt. He
launched an attack upon one of their retainers in Middle Egypt,
and—at least as he tells the story—it was so successful that he
"broke down [the enemy's] walls, killed his people, and made his
wife come down to the riverbank [as part of the loot]. My soldiers
were as lions!" It was the beginning of the end of Hyksos
domination.

Kamose lived in the final days of the Seventeenth Dynasty,
the first quarter of the sixteenth century B.C. Egypt was finally
emerging from the sad years of dynasties thirteen to sixteen,
years in which she languished first under feeble pharaohs and
then under foreign overlords. His victorious attack was matched

*Attended by his mother, Amenhotep III holds a royal crook, mace, and flail—
the traditional emblems of pharaonic power in the fourteenth century B.C.*

Peasants beneath an arbor harvest grapes for wine, to be savored at banquets. This scene and the one opposite are from the Theban tomb of a fourteenth-century-B.C. scribe named Nakht.

by others, as the Egyptians' revolt gathered momentum. The final triumph was achieved by an able military commander named Ahmose, also of Thebes: he led the armies that thrust the Hyksos out of the land once and for all. About 1576 he was crowned pharaoh, the first of the Eighteenth Dynasty. It was to include some of the celebrated names in Egyptian history, rulers who carried her arms far beyond her borders and made her for a time the mightiest empire of the ancient world.

Ahmose's soldiers triumphed by fighting the devil with fire, by learning to use the new Asiatic instruments of war—body armor, powerful bow, horse and chariot—and turning them against their oppressors. Egypt, having tasted victory, kept right on going, particularly under the hard-driving Thutmose I (1530–1517). His predecessors had recaptured most of the land the pharaohs of the Middle Kingdom once held in the south; he pushed on to the Fourth Cataract, while, to the north, he fought his way right up to Syria. His son Thutmose II campaigned in both Nubia and Palestine—and then Egypt's aggressions came to a halt.

The halt was brought about by Hatshepsut, the first woman to reign as pharaoh in her own right and the first great queen in recorded history. She had by blood as legitimate a claim to the succession as there could be: she was daughter of Thutmose I and half-sister of Thutmose II, who was at the same time her husband. Such marriages were not uncommon.

When Thutmose II died, she grasped the reins of government as regent during the minority of his heir, Thutmose III, a child he had fathered by a subordinate wife in the harem. With a sure political touch, Hatshepsut built up a powerful following of faithful retainers and maintained herself on the throne for the rest of her lifetime, from 1504 to 1483. There had been earlier Egyptian queens who ruled alone, but always as a temporary substitute for a male heir. Hatshepsut ruled as pharaoh: her statues portray her with a crown on her head, masculine dress on her body, and on her chin the pharaoh's traditional false beard.

Hatshepsut preferred acts of peace to acts of war. One of these acts of peace is particularly well known because she was so proud of it she had it pictured on her temple in a series of delicately carved reliefs. She had dispatched a trading expedition to the land of Punt, as Egyptians called what is now the eastern part of the Sudan, from the highlands to the shores of the Red Sea. The prime purpose was to secure incense, for which Punt was the major source. The carvings show the sleek clean-lined galleys of Hatshepsut's flotilla entering the harbor at Punt; then her royal messenger and a file of his men with objects of barter—necklaces, hatchets, daggers—to offer to the local chieftain, who advances followed by an enormously fat wife, two sons, and a daughter. Then, farther along, there is frenetic activity as a line of Puntites load the ships with myrrh—live myrrh trees with their roots carefully bagged—and other items of the region such as rare woods, ivory, cattle. The scenes have captions: "Hard to port," calls the pilot of one of the vessels as they maneuver; "Watch your step!" is carved over the stevedores doing the loading; and surely there is a flash of Egyptian humor in the label "the ass which carries his wife" over the meek little donkey that trots in the wake of the massive queen.

Hatshepsut held on to the throne, keeping in a subordinate position a man who would prove to be the most forceful and daring pharaoh Egypt ever had. When she died, Thutmose III came into his own—and paid her off by obliterating her name from every public monument where it appeared. Then he spun the ship of state about and set out on the pre-Hatshepsut course—foreign conquest.

Thutmose III was Egypt's Napoleon. Under him the empire reached its high-water mark, to the south beyond the Fourth Cataract and to the north as far as the upper border of Syria. Palestine and Lebanon became Egyptian protectorates. In Old Kingdom days Egypt, which is virtually treeless, had to buy the timber for shipbuilding at Byblos, whose merchants offered for sale the wood of the famed cedars of Lebanon. Now she could commandeer all she wanted; as Thutmose put it: "Every year

Four attendants bear symbolic offerings for Nakht and his wife, who was buried with him. The scribe's hoard for the afterlife includes ducks, fish, grapes, cucumbers, eggs, and figs.

there is hewn [for me] ... genuine cedar of Lebanon, which is brought to the court." His new possessions offered yet another item in short supply back home: big game, especially elephants, which were still to be found in Syria in his day. He boasts of having hunted down no less than 120.

The Egypt of these swift-moving times was a far cry from what it had been under the Old Kingdom. Then it had been an isolated land, an Egypt for the Egyptians. Now colonies of Egyptians made their homes in Palestine and Lebanon; Egyptian garrisons were stationed in every major town there. And foreigners from varied lands were an everyday sight on Egypt's streets—traders from Asia, mercenaries from Libya or Nubia, enslaved captives from the lands she had conquered. A complicated bureaucracy was needed to run this enlarged imperial nation. The pharaohs of the Eighteenth Dynasty, natives of Thebes, which lies far up the river, elected to make it their capital. To handle the northern part of the country an administrator called vizier of Lower Egypt was appointed, who governed from the former Old Kingdom capital at Memphis. To handle the conquered territory to the south there was a viceroy of Ethiopia, who represented the pharaoh. And since the pharaohs spent so much time away on campaign, there was also a vizier of Upper Egypt to take care of the government at Thebes.

He must have had his hands full. From a sleepy provincial town Thebes suddenly had been promoted to the capital of an empire. Thebes became a veritable boomtown as the pharaohs hurriedly raised new palaces to house the swelling bureaucracy and new temples to honor the gods who had smiled on Egypt's endeavors. One deity profited above all the others—Amen. For long he had been only an obscure Theban god. The Middle Kingdom pharaohs, who came from Thebes, first raised him to prominence, and the pharaohs of the Eighteenth Dynasty, crediting him with the success of Egypt's arms, erected grandiose temples for his worship. The temples still stand, though lacking the treasures—the furniture of rare woods, the offering vessels of

Explorers set sail for Punt to fetch exotic goods for Hatshepsut in this limestone relief, which like the one below, is from the pharaoh's temple. The ship, one of many in the expedition, is powered by sail and oar.

The king and queen of Punt welcome Egyptian traders and, in a seemingly lopsided arrangement, exchange incense and other luxuries for trinkets. The inscriptions say that the Egyptians ridiculed the obese queen.

Hatshepsut, the first woman pharaoh to rule Egypt entirely on her own, wears a pharaoh's ceremonial beard in this limestone sphinx, which guarded the highest tier of her mortuary temple. Hatshepsut's portraits in the traditional male costume of the pharaoh left no doubt that she wielded ultimate power over Upper and Lower Egypt.

A WOMAN TAKES THE THRONE

Egypt's traditions held that only a man could be pharaoh, but in 1504 B.C., Queen Hatshepsut, whose official portrait is at left, seized power and ruled the Nile kingdom for twenty-one years.

Pharaonic scepter in hand, she restored peace to a warring Egypt, revitalized foreign trade, and ordered construction projects throughout the country, including the restoration of ancient temples. She also erected a grand, triple-terraced mortuary temple for herself, which stands majestically against the cliffs at Deir al-Bahri, on the western side of Thebes. The temple, a complex of colonnaded shrines connected by great ramps, is distinct from the monolithic nature of most ancient Egyptian architecture.

Reliefs in the enormous temple immortalize her life and deeds, including scenes from an expedition she dispatched to the land of Punt, in what is today eastern Sudan (details of the scenes are opposite). Hatshepsut masterminded this arduous trade mission to acquire new supplies of ebony, ivory, gold, leopard skins, and myrrh. But Hatshepsut's successor, the once-deposed Thutmose III, demolished many of his stepmother's monuments and claimed the years of her illustrious reign as his own.

precious metals—that once filled them. The palaces have disappeared. All that remain are the outlines of their ground plan.

There are no mighty pyramids dotting the landscape around Thebes as there are around Giza and Sakkara and other burial sites of the earlier kings. This was not because the pharaohs of the Eighteenth or later dynasties were less powerful or less wealthy. It was because Egypt by now had lived through two extended periods of unrest, civil war, and lawlessness—first the period that brought the Old Kingdom to an end, then the one that did the same for the Middle Kingdom. And these had left practically every tomb in sight stripped of its treasures.

A pharaoh or noble still had to be buried surrounded by his precious possessions—to do otherwise was unthinkable—but why in the open topped by a marker that would attract robbers as sure as honey does flies? From Thutmose I on, pharaohs were laid to rest in vaults hacked out of the living rock within the so-called Valley of the Kings. The typical royal tomb now consisted of a long corridor that, slanting downward into the heart of the earth, led to a series of chambers in which were placed the pharaoh's coffin and his multitude of belongings. The nobles' tombs, in the Theban hills, were similar, but much more modest.

As in Old Kingdom times, tomb walls were decorated with scenes from daily life. Many of them were now done in paint rather than in relief. Once the body was deposited inside, the entrance was sealed up and, at least in the case of royal tombs, left unmarked. The point was to render the spot as unobtrusive as possible. As the architect of Thutmose I put it: "I saw to the digging out of the hill-sepulcher of His Majesty privily, none seeing and hearing."

The precautions were no help: in the course of the centuries, these rocky fastnesses were robbed as ruthlessly as their conspicuous predecessors. The pictures on the walls give us an idea of the riches the plunderers must have made off with. Alongside scenes of farming, herding, craftsmen at work, and the like,

A maid, at left above, offers refreshment and a linen napkin to a lady seated at a banquet. All of the elegant guests—talking among themselves and passing flowers around—wear perfumed cones atop their elaborate wigs. This scene is from a fourteenth-century-B.C. tomb at Thebes.

there are banquets and court ceremonials, occasions when the participants presumably were dressed in their very best. The high and mighty appear there so loaded with jewelry one wonders how they supported it all: crowns, necklaces that cover the whole upper chest, broad bracelets and armlets and anklets, heavy drop earrings.

People wore jewelry even during humdrum moments at home. Young girls, for example, or at least those in the paintings, went around the house without a stitch of clothing—but with earrings and clusters of armlets, anklets, and necklaces. The pharaohs rewarded deserving officials by bestowing upon them golden chains; one relief shows a famous general carrying at least half a dozen around his neck, the Egyptian equivalent of a breastful of medals. Jewelry was set with the same stones favored in earlier days, notably turquoise and lapis lazuli.

How much treasure these tombs contained—and at the same time how and why they were forever being robbed—is strikingly revealed by a set of papyrus documents that were discovered during the last century. They date to about 1120 B.C., almost two centuries after the end of the flourishing Eighteenth Dynasty, an age when Egypt once again had fallen upon hard times. Among other matters, they contain the report of a special government inquiry the pharaoh had launched.

On the basis of the evidence gathered, the vizier at Thebes declared that ten tombs of kings, four of queens, and many of the nobles had been broken into, and he brought charges against two suspects, a coppersmith and a stonemason. The documents include the stonemason's deposition at his trial. He tells how he and his seven accomplices tunneled into the tomb—his training as a mason no doubt stood him in good stead—and stripped the mummies of the pharaoh and his queen of their gold and silver ornaments and costly gems, and then set fire to the coffin. "And," he goes on, "we made the gold which we had found on these two gods—from their mummies, amulets, ornaments, and coffins—into eight shares. And twenty *deben* of gold fell to each

With a double flute, a long-necked lute, and a harp, three ladies make music for Nakht, whose tomb walls they adorn. Such troupes of musicians entertained at many lavish parties.

one of the eight of us, making one hundred sixty *deben* of gold"— in other words, a total take of about forty pounds, with the members of the gang getting close to five per man.

The next part of the deposition reveals that one of today's pernicious problems in law enforcement—corruption of the enforcers—is age-old: "The agents of Thebes heard that we had been stealing ... so they arrested me and imprisoned me at the Mayor of Thebes' place. So I took the twenty *deben* of gold that had fallen to me as [my] share, and gave them to Kha-em-opet, the District Clerk ... He let me go, and I joined my companions, and they made up for me another share. And I, as well as the other robbers who are with me, have continued to this day in the practice of robbing the tombs..." Why not? The hauls were so rich that, even if a man was caught, he could bribe his way out and still have plenty left over.

But this was one time when cold-eyed planning did not work out. Not only were the stonemason and his accomplices brought up to trial but so were a considerable number of others that the Egyptian authorities were able to round up. Of the culprits, fifteen were executed, fifteen sent to jail, and only two let go.

But such robberies lay centuries ahead. There were no shadows on the horizon when, in 1401 B.C., Pharaoh Amenhotep III ascended the throne. His reign was long, almost forty years, and during its peaceful later years he had no need to follow in the footsteps of his athletic and bellicose predecessors. Instead of chasing enemies or big game, he was able to loll in munificence in resplendent surroundings. Instead of spending time and money on campaigns, he spent them on ambitious building projects, including a grandiose new palace at Thebes whose grounds boasted a man-made lake a mile and a half long. He broke with tradition by marrying Tiy, a woman without a trace of royal blood, making her his queen.

Yet his breaks with tradition were as nothing compared with his son's. These introduced Egypt to a disconcerting experience she had hitherto been spared: heresy.

THE IMPERIAL HIGH LIFE

This golden lion, the royal beast of Egypt, was buried with King Ahmose. The father of the New Kingdom, Ahmose brought great opulence to Egyptian court life.

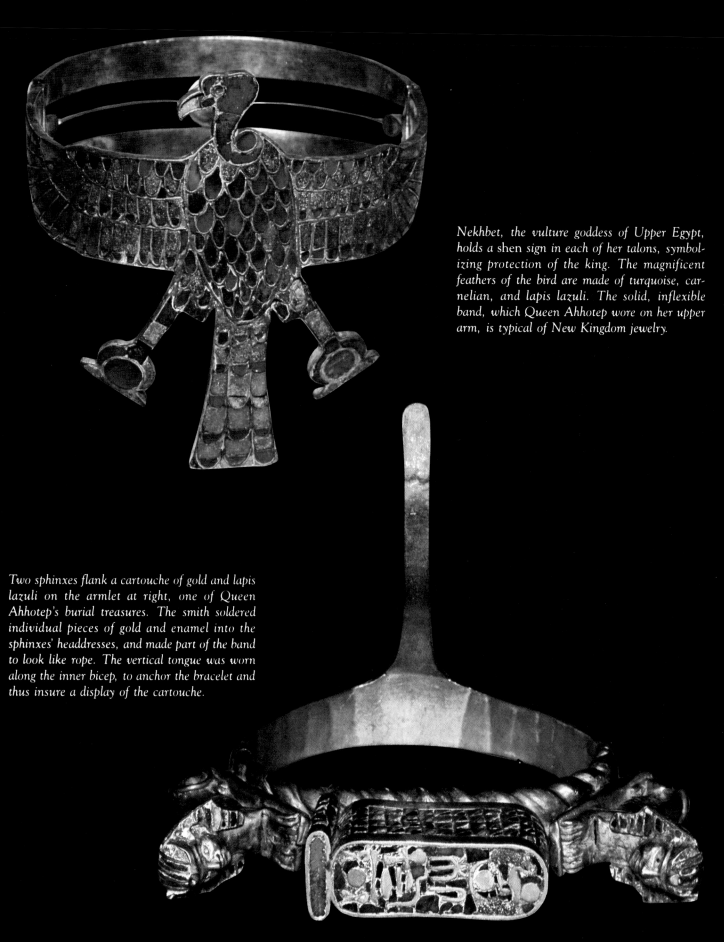

Nekhbet, the vulture goddess of Upper Egypt, holds a shen sign in each of her talons, symbolizing protection of the king. The magnificent feathers of the bird are made of turquoise, carnelian, and lapis lazuli. The solid, inflexible band, which Queen Ahhotep wore on her upper arm, is typical of New Kingdom jewelry.

Two sphinxes flank a cartouche of gold and lapis lazuli on the armlet at right, one of Queen Ahhotep's burial treasures. The smith soldered individual pieces of gold and enamel into the sphinxes' headdresses, and made part of the band to look like rope. The vertical tongue was worn along the inner bicep, to anchor the bracelet and thus insure a display of the cartouche.

Ahmose's coronation is commemorated in this gold and lapis lazuli bracelet of Queen Ahhotep.

Egypt entered her grand imperial age in 1576 B.C., with the founding of the Eighteenth Dynasty by Queen Ahhotep's two sons, Ahmose and Kamose. Expanding the empire into Syria, Palestine, and the Sudan, succeeding generations of the ruling families—from Ahmose to Thutmose III to Amenhotep III—brought prosperity to all of Egypt and a magnificent court life to the palaces of Thebes.

With the proceeds of their victories, the royal Egyptians indulged expensive tastes for precious jewelry (which they wore every day), exotic perfumes and incense, and silver, which was not to be found in Egypt. Cabinetmakers created furniture out of fine imported woods. Pampered women spent idle days fixing one an-other's coiffures, arranging flowers, and applying cosmetics before gilded mirrors. Musicians and dancers entertained the privileged Egyptians at banquets, while servants brought food on silver platters and wine in turquoise-colored goblets.

In addition to parties, the Egyptians enjoyed boating on the Nile, picnics, and quiet games of senet, a fashionable board game. They placed great value on the possessions of their ancestors, and collected heirloom pieces, which instead of taking to their tombs they passed on to their descendants.

After such splendid lives, the royal families of the Eighteenth Dynasty ended their days in grand, treasure-filled tombs.

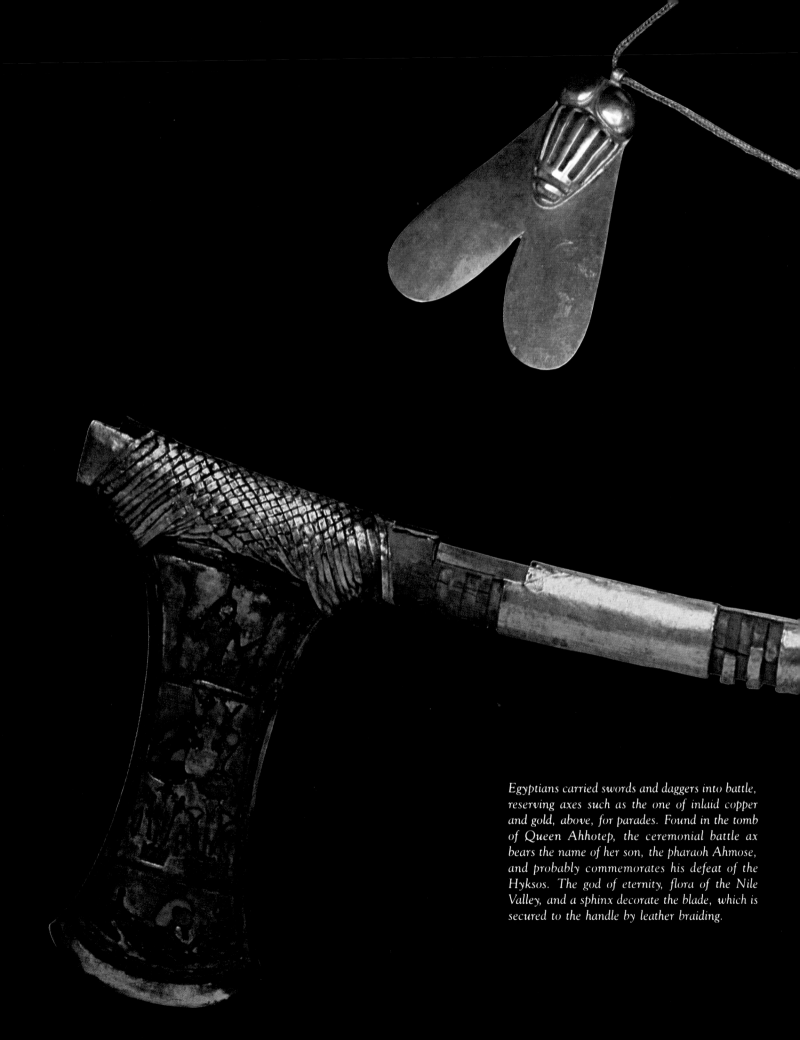

Egyptians carried swords and daggers into battle, reserving axes such as the one of inlaid copper and gold, above, for parades. Found in the tomb of Queen Ahhotep, the ceremonial battle ax bears the name of her son, the pharaoh Ahmose, and probably commemorates his defeat of the Hyksos. The god of eternity, flora of the Nile Valley, and a sphinx decorate the blade, which is secured to the handle by leather braiding.

Queen Ahhotep frequently bestowed military honors such as this necklace of golden flies, a decoration for valor. To the Egyptians, an exemplary soldier was like a fly, persistently swarming around enemies. The realism of the flies' eyes, bodies, and wings was heightened by an eerie effect: as the decorated soldier moved about, light bouncing off the gold medals reproduced the natural iridescence of the insects.

When important Egyptians sat down to dinner, they usually did so at individual tables, while lesser mortals ate at their feet. The three Syrian wives of Thutmose III—Menhet, Menwi, and Merti—were three such privileged persons, and in about 1460 B.C., the pharaoh himself gave each woman matching sets of the tableware seen here. The silver canister below and silver cup opposite were particularly special treasures since silver, unlike gold—used to make the bowl opposite—was rare throughout Egypt. The turquoise-colored goblet is one of the earliest glass vessels known.

SILVER CANISTER

54

SILVER CUP

GLASS GOBLET

GOLD BOWL

55

These golden funeral slippers, worn by one of King Thutmose III's Syrian wives, imitate everyday wicker sandals. All three women were buried in such footwear and with gold jewelry, including the armlet at left.

Red and gold lions, lying between barrel beads of gold and lapis lazuli, form the outer plaque of an armlet. King Thutmose III gave each of his Syrian wives identical armlets, and each of the ladies chose to be buried with hers. This one was recovered from their harem tomb, sealed in the fifteenth century B.C.

Amenhotep III accepts emblems of long life from two of his daughters in this relief of carnelian stone from a bracelet. The king and his queen Tiy sit in palanquins for a celebratory procession during his first jubilee.

Leisure-loving Egyptian aristocrats played senet, a board game of luck and skill. The rules of the game are a mystery, but the object seems to have been to move the eight pieces across and off the board, according to chance throws of dice or sticks. Enthusiasts of senet took the game to their graves, so they could play it throughout eternity. Amenhotep III is thought to have owned this game board of wood and blue-glazed earthenware.

A statue of a concubine (opposite) from the harem of King Amenhotep III faces its reflection in a mirror. With her elaborate black wig, scented head cone, and full lips, the painted ivory figure is the ideal of a New Kingdom consort. The tiny statue (it is less than four inches tall) is probably an heirloom of the royal family.

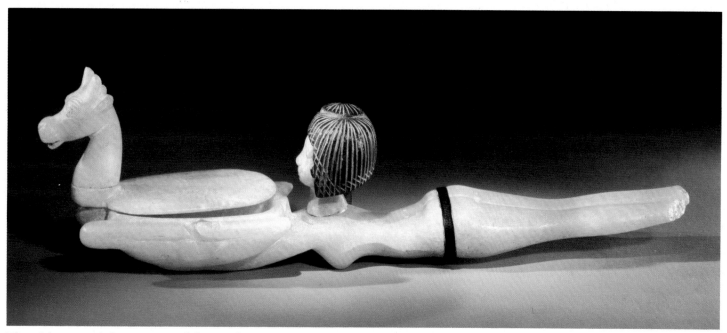

This alabaster and slate cosmetic dish is made in the form of a swimming gazelle, its back hollowed out, pulling a girl through water.

OVERLEAF: When Amenhotep III dispatched news, he did so by issuing scarabs, such as this one (both sides of the beetle are shown). It announces the opening of a lake and pleasure garden the pharaoh built for Queen Tiy and her guests, whom she entertained with picnics, parties, and cruises. The Egyptians associated the scarab with the sun and used the motif in their art and treasures. This beetle, which carried the news of the plush resort to members of the pharaoh's court and the privileged citizens of Thebes, is made of green-glazed stone.

III

THE ECCENTRIC ROYAL COUPLE

AKHENATEN AND NEFERTITI

When his son and successor was born, sometime before 1363 B.C., Amenhotep III gave the child his own name. Meaning "Amen is satisfied," it was a favorite among members of the Eighteenth Dynasty; Amen, after all, was the one god they revered above every other. There had been two Amenhoteps before, and the new arrival was the fourth.

Everybody—at least everybody whose opinion mattered: the royal family, nobles, clergy, bureaucracy—assumed that Amenhotep IV would follow in the footsteps of his predecessors, would shine at court like his father or on the battlefield like his grandfather or in some other equally pharaonic way.

He came to the throne in 1363, and for a number of years behaved more or less as expected. He married a certain Nefertiti. The name means "the beautiful one is come," and if her portraits are true to life, it could not be more apt. She was an eminently proper choice, for she had royal blood in her veins—though exactly whose is not known. The guesses run the gamut, with

Unlike earlier pharaohs, the reformer Akhenaten openly showed affection for his family. He and wife Nefertiti (on the right) fondle three of their daughters.

Akhenaten's mother, Queen Tiy, here sculpted in boxwood, was active in state affairs early in her son's reign. She also supported his religious fervor, and in gratitude Akhenaten erected a temple for her in his elegant new capital at Amarna.

some experts claiming that she was Amenhotep IV's very own sister and others that she was not even Egyptian but a foreign princess from the court of Egypt's most powerful northern neighbor, the Mitanni, who lived around the upper Euphrates. Shortly after the marriage, Nefertiti bore her husband the first of six daughters. Pictures of him from these years show him in the time-honored fashion of the pharaohs, with trim athletic figure in a regal pose.

But it soon became apparent that Amenhotep IV was very much his own man. He was an intellectual, the sole pharaoh in Egypt's history to boast that distinction. As such, he had advanced ideas concerning women. His father had started a new trend by giving the queen some prominence in official pictures; the son went much further, having his artists include in scene after scene not only Nefertiti but some of their daughters as well. He liked to write poetry, and at least one of his efforts, a hymn of about one hundred fifty lines, has survived:

> How plentiful it is, what you have made,
> although they are hidden from view,
> sole god, without another beside you;
> you created the earth as you wished,
> when you were by yourself [before]
> mankind, all cattle and kine,
> all beings on land, who fare upon their feet,
> and all beings in the air, who fly with their wings.

The poem is amazingly reminiscent of the 104th Psalm. The language of the two works is in places so strikingly similar—one of the Egyptian verses is the precise equivalent of the psalmist's "How manifold are thy works!"—that scholars have wondered whether the words of an Egyptian pharaoh could possibly have reached a Hebrew poet who lived six to seven centuries later.

The poem has to be a hymn, because the one subject that engrossed the attention of this young intellectual, which eventually became an obsession, was religion. He quickly made it evident that he had no interest in Amen, the god whose name he carried, the god his ancestors had elevated to divine supremacy. He seemed much more interested in another of Egypt's multitudinous deities, the Aten, the disk of the sun. Re, the sun, was one of the country's oldest and most respected gods, and the Aten was simply the visible aspect of the sun, the giver of life, who makes the "Kine prance on their feet, and the fishes in the river leap," as the new pharaoh's hymn proclaimed. Two generations of pharaohs had already venerated the Aten.

But Amenhotep IV's veneration was much more intense. Not long after becoming pharaoh he built the Aten a new temple that he set up just east of the most grandiose of Amen's temples at Karnak, two miles north of Thebes. In this new temple he included a series of colossal statues of himself that must have hit contemporaries like a thunderbolt, so violent was its break with the past. Instead of the trim athletic figure in traditional garments he had his sculptors put him in unconventional garb and give him an egg-shaped head with elongated jaw, a scrawny neck, drooping shoulders, potbelly, spindly shanks, and buttocks as thick and round as a woman's.

Did he actually look like that? The features are almost grotesque, but there must be an element of truth in the portrayal; his poetry reveals that ma'at—"truth"—was his watchword. And this physique of his may well be one of the reasons why his career was to be so different. How could a man with such a body go in for the pharaoh's customary pursuits of destroying enemies or big game? And since he had intellectual leanings rather than the sensual tastes of his father, the luxuries of the court and the harem held no appeal. In any event, in that curious body lived a spirit so daring and imaginative it produced a phenomenon unique in Egypt's hidebound annals, a revolutionary religious reformer.

The portraits in this outré style were not just his personal way of showing himself. They were official policy. We can see this baldly and clearly in the tomb of a high-ranking official,

Ay, a high official loyal to Akhenaten, may be the subject of this plaster mask. Commander of the king's cavalry as well as a scribe, he eventually attained the throne himself after the death of Akhenaten's successor, Tutankhamen.

Ramose, vizier of Upper Egypt. As one would expect from so important a figure, Ramose had a magnificent burial chamber prepared for himself, the walls decorated with the usual scenes portraying especially happy moments in his life. In two of these the pharaoh appears; in one Amenhotep is receiving flowers from Ramose, and in the other he presents an award to his faithful servitor. In the first, the pharaoh looks like any traditional Egyptian ruler. In the second, done sometime later, he is in his new guise.

In the sixth year of his reign, Amenhotep IV took a critical step: he shook off the dust of Thebes and transferred the capital elsewhere. It was a virtual declaration of independence. Thebes was Amen's city: his two greatest temples stood there, and the army of clergy who tended him lived there. How could one worship another god in Amen's awesome shadow? So the pharaoh left and set up a new capital 250 miles downriver at a spot ideal for planting a settlement. On the east bank the mountains recede to form a crescent-shaped plain some eight miles long and three broad; here the city was built. Across the river from it was an even ampler plain; here were grown the crops needed to feed the denizens. He named the place Akhetaten, "the horizon of the Aten"; historians call it Amarna, from the name of the modern village nearby. At the same time he changed his own name to Akhenaten. No longer was he to be "Amen is satisfied" but "the effective spirit of the Aten." The Aten, in short, was to replace Amen as the supreme god of the land.

At the heart of the new city rose a sunlit temple to the Aten. Surrounding it were the royal palace and the administration buildings, an elegant residential section for the nobility and a humbler one for the rank and file, workshops, and the like. Near the cliffs that overlooked the city was a hastily set up housing complex for the architects, engineers, masons, and painters who went immediately to work hacking out burial chambers for the pharaoh and his court.

In his new capital Akhenaten was free to worship his new

Akhenaten's bewigged lieutenant Ay, with his wife Ti behind him, accepts a collar of gold handed down by the pharaoh from the Window of Appearances—a palace portal where the royal family would honor their favorites before the public.

deity. Carvings discovered at Amarna reveal the very special way the worshiping was done. They show the Aten with rays that end in hands stretching downward toward Akhenaten and his family; all about are courtiers who bow humbly, very humbly, in reverence. Akhenaten prayed to the Aten, and everybody else prayed to Akhenaten; there was no god save the one god, and the sole way to get to him was through Akhenaten. At some point Akhenaten translated this egocentric monotheism of his into effective action: he sent men armed with chisels up and down the country to strike out the offending name of Amen wherever they found it.

What Akhenaten created was a form of monotheism, the very first example in the history of religion. But it was not the monotheism that was destined to live on; that arose centuries later among the Jews. Akhenaten's monotheism died with him. For one, it was a religion of the intellect; it had no ethical conviction to fire people's souls, to inspire passionate devotees. It was a palace religion, available only to those near enough to Akhenaten to count on his intercession.

Amen's clergy did not transfer to the new capital. They stayed behind at Thebes, fuming and plotting. Of the nobility, some stayed behind and some elected to follow Akhenaten and continue to serve in his government, though how many and of what status is unclear. Whoever they were, they must have enjoyed as much luxury at Amarna as at Thebes. Unfortunately, whatever precious objects they owned have been irretrievably lost: when Akhenaten's strange interlude came to an end, the place was abandoned, and the buildings and tombs became natural targets for scavengers.

Yet, amid the ruins of Amarna archaeologists have found treasure—not treasure of silver and gold and costly gems, but artistic treasure, the paintings and sculptures that once adorned the buildings and tombs. They reveal an art of a special nature, strikingly unlike anything that had gone before. In his new capital Akhenaten had himself portrayed with his peculiar

TEXT CONTINUED ON PAGE 78

BEAUTY IN THE ROUND

Sculptors' studios at Amarna yielded these three heads of Nefertiti. The limestone bust (right), painted and with a headdress, may have served as a model for the two rough versions in sandstone (center) and quartzite (left).

Nothing more epitomized all that was lovely in Amarna than Akhenaten's wife Queen Nefertiti. That she became legendary is a tribute to the gifted workmanship of the Amarna sculptors. As remnants from their studios reveal, these craftsmen possessed an incomparable skill at portraying the royal family, above all the queen, in splendid life-size statuary.

Departing from the artistic canons of previous reigns, which showed people in stiff, formal poses, sculptors working under the maverick pharaoh developed a freer style in their portraiture. Some of the faces are astonishingly lifelike; bodies are relaxed and often sensual.

Another of their innovations was to create statues by a composite method, with specialists carving only a particular part of the figure for final assembly. And for striking effect, they would fashion the parts from stones of different colors. Much of the sculptured remains, even if not damaged, are incomplete. But the pieces, like these here and on pages 74 to 77, are often exquisite in themselves. The greatest are the portraits of Nefertiti, which the artists refined into an enduring ideal of femininity. Though her likeness is 3,300 years old, the high cheekbones, long neck, and large eyes give it a quality that seems completely modern.

Even though unfinished, this quartzite portrait of Nefertiti—which bears sculptor's guidelines on the nose and brow—captures the youthful queen's radiance.

A QUEEN'S HEAD

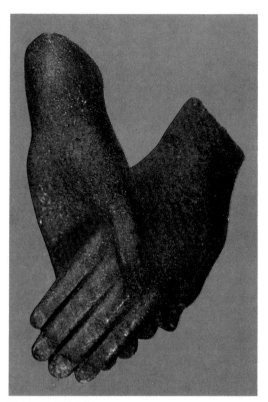

CLASPED HANDS

These spectacular fragments probably came from statues of the royal family, which either were damaged accidentally or shattered by reactionaries following Akhenaten's death and the restoration of the old order. The pharaoh's mother, Queen Tiy, was the likely model for the mouth and chin on the opposite page, part of a head carved from yellow jasper. The sculptor formed her lips to perfection, and the polished surface of the stone exudes opulence. Hard marblelike limestone is the material of the nose and mouth at right, which undoubtedly portrayed Akhenaten; the bulbous features are characteristic of many of the king's completed portraits. Like both heads, the quartzite hands above were made separately, and then attached to statuary, maybe of Akhenaten and Nefertiti or perhaps of the king and one of his daughters.

AKHENATEN

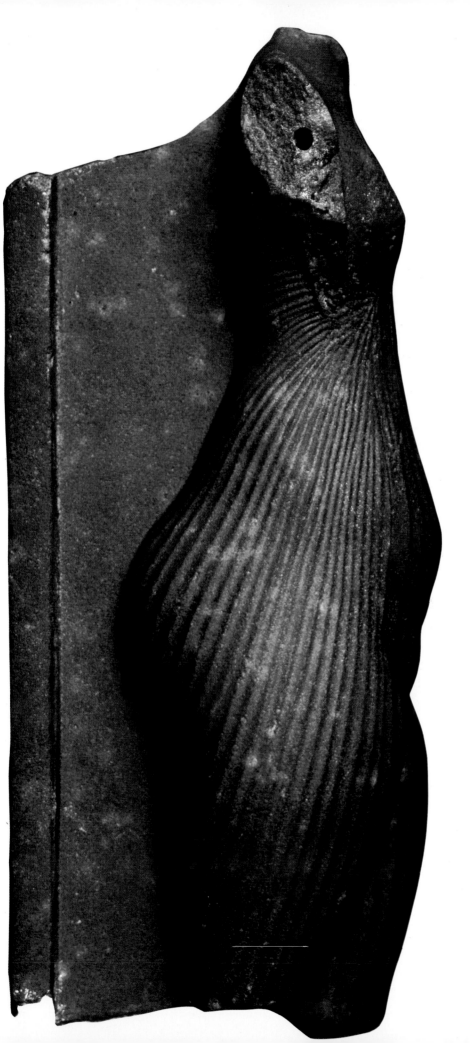

Carved from dark red quartzite by master hands, this torso of Nefertiti, in two views, is as voluptuous as that of any Greek goddess. The artist has draped the figure in a tight, pleated gown that fully reveals her luxuriant curves. The heavy buttocks and the shape of the slender waist emphasize the sensuality of the queen.

TEXT CONTINUED FROM PAGE 71

characteristics, but now they are grossly exaggerated: the neck is scrawnier than ever, the curves of the body are more feminine than ever, the legs are mere pipestems. These characteristics became elements in a standard court style: painters and sculptors dutifully gave egg-heads and elongated jaws to Akhenaten's daughters and even made his courtiers look like the pharaoh, no doubt following their instructions.

The scenes mark an equally sharp break with tradition. Hitherto the pharaoh had always appeared in properly solemn or heroic actions: towering over all the mortals in the picture, like a Gulliver among Lilliputians, he makes offerings to the gods or smites enemies or destroys prides of lions. Anything private or intimate had been scrupulously avoided. But in the court pictures that Akhenaten commissioned, the private and intimate is just what is shown: the king cradling and kissing one of his baby daughters, the queen dandling one baby on her lap while another on her shoulder plays with her crown, a princess sprawling languidly and nibbling on a cooked duck, a princess caressing her sister. All these elements add up to what is called the Amarna style, a style responsible for some of the masterpieces of Egyptian art.

From Old Kingdom days on, Egyptian art had followed a well-marked narrow path. It was formal, stylized, conservative; it sought to express abiding truths rather than catch the fleeting moment. It represented the pharaoh as massive and impressive and in a limited repertory of poses—a figure of enduring might and majesty. Lesser beings or animals occur in stylized groups and units such as never occur in nature. If one donkey stubbornly holds up a procession, the others are in as straight a line as a file of soldiers; if two girls are pulling each other's hair, their faces are in profile and their torsos in frontal view, since that was the way Egyptians traditionally rendered a figure.

Akhenaten revolutionized the rules of art as he had those of religion. Artists earlier had taken some steps in the direction of a greater naturalism, but nothing compared with the gigantic

Carrying a heavy caldron, this barefooted servant with shaved head kneels before his master. An Egyptian noble's house was staffed by a multitude of free servants and by slaves who were usually war captives or refugees.

78

strides they made under Akhenaten. They now put figures in easy poses and natural groupings. The women, for example, who mourn Ramose's death in a painting on the wall of his tomb are not in the traditional stiff ranks but in a jumbled cluster and their torsos are in profile as well as their faces. Alongside old ritualistic scenes are fresh ones observed from nature: a kingfisher in a swooping dive, ducks taking fright and fluttering out of a patch of reeds, young bulls romping among the reeds. And in representations of the royal family, the artists give us informal, intimate actions in a way unparalleled in Egyptian art. The sculptured heads reveal their own departure from tradition. In the portrait statues of Nefertiti, for example, the sloping lines, elongated neck, and dreamy expression belong unmistakably to the Amarna age.

The artists could go too far. Some pictures of Akhenaten, in which his peculiarities are almost caricatured, are grotesque. But their best efforts produced works that are not only precious but also rare, for the Amarna age lasted but a few decades and, once it was over, Egypt soon returned to the formality and stylization she was so comfortable with.

The great experiment could not last. It depended wholly upon the genius and will of one man and, when he died, it was bound to end—though just how is obscure. Unquestionably he had to contend with widespread opposition; what reformer does not? And Egypt in particular was a nation with a formidable commitment to traditional ways. After some fourteen years on the throne, during which the opposition must have steadily hardened, he was buffeted by a series of family misfortunes: the death of one or possibly more of his daughters and the death—or disgrace—of his beautiful wife. During the years at Amarna she may have fallen into disfavor, but no one knows why.

These disasters may all have proved too much for him. Exactly when he died is unknown. Suddenly he is no longer there, and Smenkhare, a younger half-brother of Akhenaten and also his son-in-law, since Smenkhare had married Akhenaten's eldest

A Nubian servant girl, her hair in a sidelock, supports a pot on her hip. This statuette, like the one on the opposite page, served as a container for unguents or cosmetics; both are outfitted with lids to secure the contents.

Draped in a sheer robe, a well-rounded Merytaten (right), eldest daughter of Akhenaten, offers flowers to her husband, Smenkhare, in this painted relief. Akhenaten named his son-in-law as coregent, but both of them died shortly afterward.

daughter, is pharaoh. He himself died within two years, and the throne passed to yet another member of Akhenaten's family, a boy of ten named Tutankhaten, later called Tutankhamen.

With the accession of Tutankhamen the clock was turned back. Pharaoh and court quit Akhenaten's new city and returned to Thebes. Amen resumed his status as the supreme god of Egypt, and the Aten retreated into obscurity. The opposition's triumph was complete.

Ancient Egypt, dedicated to the upholding of its age-old ways, was no place for mavericks. Akhenaten was the only pharaoh who ever stepped out of line, and his vanquishers did their best to efface his name from the nation's memory. Soon after his death the chisel-wielders reappeared on the scene, this time to hack out Akhenaten's name as assiduously as they had earlier hacked out Amen's.

It was the Egyptologists who rescued Akhenaten from oblivion. His enemies who consigned him there by bringing the capital back to Thebes and decreeing the abandonment of Akhenaten's new city, did posterity a favor. Amarna, desolate and empty, was covered over with sand. When the excavators sank their spades in the place some thirty-two centuries later they struck archaeological treasure.

In the ruins of the palace they came upon fragments of the lovely paintings that once adorned the walls. In the studios of the sculptors they came upon lovely portrait heads, some of which had not yet been completed when their fashioners dropped their tools and left for Thebes. In the unfinished tombs in the cliffs behind the town and in the nearly empty royal tomb up a side valley—only Akhenaten's second daughter, who died very young, was buried there—they came upon carvings and inscriptions. All this enabled them to piece together the story of this king whom Egypt wanted to forget—and to resurrect works of art that have been universally acclaimed as treasures.

THE RADICAL'S SPLENDID CITY

A deftly carved swag of geese dangles from a column on this limestone block—one of the magnificent reliefs that adorned palaces and temples at Amarna.

Though a religious idealist, Pharaoh Akhenaten was no ascetic, and he saw to it that the chief buildings in his new capital at Amarna were lavishly decorated. Brightly colored murals covered the walls and floors of elegant villas and of the pharaoh's own private quarters. On the outside of such monuments as the Grand Palace and the half-mile-long main temple, or House of Aten, master sculptors carved hundreds of crisp reliefs in hard, white limestone.

The major subject of these ornaments was the royal family, portrayed in relaxed, domestic moments and all displaying, apparently at the insistence of Akhenaten, the king's peculiar deformities. But the Amarna artists also excelled at lively scenes of crowds, of town life, and of nature, rendering them with great vigor and attention to detail. The result, glimpsed in the fragments on these pages, was a joyous pageant designed to give pleasure as well as to honor the sun disk, the Aten. It was also a unique achievement. Echoes of the Amarna style continued into the next dynasty; but the monuments themselves, like the new faith, crumbled after the death of ancient Egypt's lone heretic.

The prominent chin, thin neck, and drooping shoulders of Akhenaten appear in sunken relief on a limestone fragment from Amarna. Traces of pigment on this piece, and on other Amarna reliefs, were probably added in modern times.

A large hand with sensitively shaped fingers, probably belonging to Akhenaten, holds out an olive branch heavy with fruit to the rays of the Aten. The rays end in tiny hands, symbolizing the love, protection, and vitality extended by the god. Olives, considered exotic, here replace the traditional bouquet of flowers as an offering. The workmanship of this relief is unusually fine: instead of appearing flat, Akhenaten's hand has the illusion of depth, an extraordinary innovation in the art of that time.

Nefertiti gently kisses one of her daughters as the beneficent hand of the Aten offers them an ankh, symbol of life. The queen wears a wig and diadem, while the child affects a long sidelock of hair that covers her ear. This scene is one of the few in Egyptian art to portray. kissing.

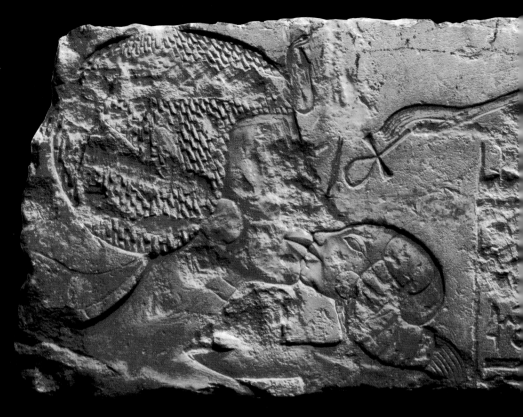

In another of the domestic scenes that delighted Akhenaten, a young princess clutches the arm of her wet nurse, whose gown is arranged to reveal her prominent breasts. Such frontal views of women were virtually unknown before the artistic revolution at Amarna.

Wearing a light pleated gown, Nefertiti sits upon the lap of her husband in this intricately carved fragment. The queen's arm supports the diminutive limbs of two of her children; to the right, resting on a stand, is a bowl filled with fruit and a bunch of flowers.

Excessively long yet elegantly modeled, these feet were part of a complete figure—certainly a royal lady and perhaps Queen Nefertiti.

Five court musicians, all women, perform with a harp, lutes, a flute, and a lyre in this relief fragment from Akhenaten's Great Palace.

A trumpeter, at right above, plays for a group of peasant women who dance excitedly—perhaps in anticipation of the pharaoh's arrival.

The graceful hands of a harp player attest to the supreme skill of the Amarna sculptors in this detail, opposite, from the orchestra scene at top.

Ducks soar skyward above a grove of swamp plants in this scene painted on the floor of one of the Amarna palaces. Detailed open-air scenes like this one, executed in muted tones, filled the main hall and were intended to be walked on as well as to beautify the building.

93

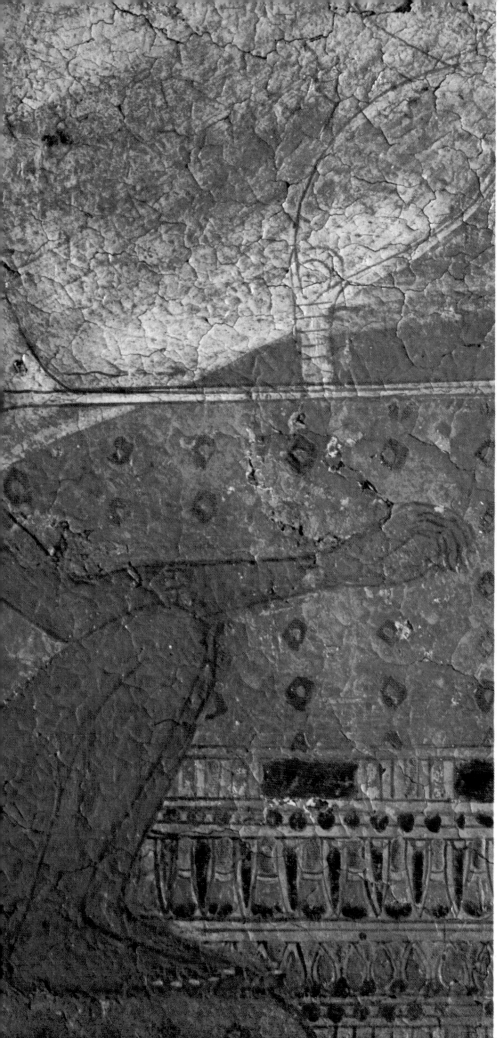

With their heads shaved and necks bejeweled, two of Akhenaten's six daughters, Neferneferuaten-tasherit and Neferneferure, caress each other while seated on brightly patterned cushions in this fragment from a palace mural. The princess at left has a left hand where her right should be, an artistic quirk harking back to pre-Amarna poses. But the children's egg-shaped heads and rounded tummies, as well as the warmth, intimacy, and grace of the scene, typify the Amarna style.

IV

THE GOLDEN BOY-KING

TUTANKHAMEN

The name Tutankhamen conjures up one thought—gold. Ancient Egypt was rich in gold. Archaeologists have found many workings with the telltale traces left by her miners. Herodotus knew how rich she was: "Ethiopia," he wrote, "bears much gold"; by Ethiopia he meant what is called today Nubia, and the deposits there did indeed bear much gold. Egypt's neighbors knew too, as is revealed by some letters in a file of correspondence that was found at Amarna: an interchange between Amenhotep III and Tushratta, king of the Mitanni, Egypt's powerful neighbor on the Euphrates.

Amenhotep had requested one of Tushratta's daughters for his harem, and Tushratta wanted to be sure to get all he could as bride-price. So he wrote to Amenhotep reminding him of how he—Amenhotep—had earlier given Tushratta's father "a great deal of gold, great offering bowls of gold, great pitchers of gold, a slab of gold." Then he launched into a complaint about the paltry amount he was being offered for his daughter from the

Leaning on his royal staff, the youthful Tutankhamen accepts bouquets of lotus and papyrus from his devoted wife, Ankhesenamen, in this scene on an ivory plaque.

king of a land where "gold is as plentiful as dust." The expression so appealed to him that he used it in a follow-up letter: "that which he wanted is more abundant than dust in Egypt."

The tomb of Tutankhamen provides the eye-filling proof of what Tushratta was talking about: the profusion of gold takes one's breath away. The king's coffin, for example, is of pure gold weighing over 240 pounds. If there were such riches in the grave of a minor pharaoh who died prematurely after a short reign, what must have been in those of Egypt's great figures, of Thutmose III or the Amenhotep to whom Tushratta wrote?

Tutankhamen is the only one of Egypt's long line of pharaohs whose name is known to the general public. He does not owe this fame to the color of his personality or to the impact he had on history or even to the impact he had on his own country. He was only a child of ten when he ascended the throne in 1347 B.C., a mere youth of eighteen when death took him off it; and for the few years he reigned, he acted under the orders of others. Fame came to him over three millennia after he had passed away, when his tomb was discovered in 1922—the only royal tomb that had escaped being stripped bare by robbers.

Everything about Tutankhamen is obscure, including his ancestry. Some authorities think he was Akhenaten's son, though not by Nefertiti, but by some lesser wife. Others think he was Akhenaten's younger brother. Amenhotep III, Akhenaten's father, lived to a vigorous old age and during all his years made happy use of his harem. Whatever the exact parentage, Tutankhamen was certainly of the royal family. Born just about the time when Akhenaten made his new form of worship official, the child was given the appropriate name of Tutankhaten, "living image of the Aten." He became Akhenaten's son-in-law by marrying his third daughter, Ankhesenpaaten. Under what circumstances he inherited the throne is a mystery, for the events surrounding Akhenaten's fall and death are shadowy.

But he did inherit it. Yet he clearly was only the nominal ruler of the land; the real rulers were those powerful members of the

Aiming his bow from a war chariot, Tutankhamen leads a charge against a scattered horde of Asiatic soldiers. It is doubtful that the young king ever actually waged war, and this painting was probably done to symbolize his, and Egypt's, invincibility.

clergy and nobility who had quenched Akhenaten's revolution. They very likely chose him since he was qualified by blood and, being so young, would do what he was told. What they told him to do was to restore Amen to the predominance from which Akhenaten had toppled him.

Thebes, the city of Amen par excellence, again became the capital. The pharaoh and his queen advertised their switch of allegiance by changing their names to Tutankhamen and Ankhesenamen (the exact reverse of what Akhenaten had done), and they made amends not only to Amen but to all the other gods for the neglect they had suffered because of the great heretic's single-minded devotion to the Aten. "When His Majesty" [a pharaoh's way of saying *I*] "appeared as king," declared Tutankhamen in an inscription he put up at Karnak, "the temples of the gods and goddesses from Elephantine [at the First Cataract] to the marshes of the delta . . . had gone to pieces. Their shrines had become desolate, had become mounds overgrown with [weeds] . . . His Majesty deliberated plans with his heart, searching for any beneficial deed, seeking out acts of service for his father Amen . . . All the [property] of the temples had been doubled, tripled, and quadrupled in silver, [gold], lapis lazuli, turquoise, every [kind of] august costly stone, royal linen, white linen, fine linen, olive oil, gum, fat . . . without limit to any good thing." The clock had been turned back for fair.

Who was pulling the strings of the puppet king? A certain Ay was important, an elder statesman who served as Tutankhamen's vizier and succeeded him as pharaoh, ruling for four years. Then there was Haremhab. He was commander of Tutankhamen's armies and became his top administrator. Eventually, as generals so often will, he seized power for himself: he was crowned pharaoh in 1334 and ruled efficiently for twenty-eight years. Despite his service under Tutankhamen and no doubt also under Akhenaten before that, Haremhab managed to disassociate himself so successfully from those two monarchs tainted by connection with the great heresy that he gained entry to the

In this detail of a tomb painting, a superintendent, at left, oversees artisans in a royal workshop. At upper right, an assistant weighs gold rings using a bronze counterweight in the shape of a bull's head. Below him, two jewelers present finished objects such as inlaid collars and bracelets.

THE NOBLEST METAL

Gold was the most favored material during the New Kingdom: it did not tarnish, it could be easily worked, and its warm color evoked the divine brilliance of the sun. Because much of the gold collected in Egypt went to the pharaoh and his nobles, the craftsmen who worked with it were a privileged community employed mostly in the royal ateliers.

The artisan enjoying the highest esteem was the *nuby*, or goldsmith, whose craft most likely remained within a few families, passed on from father to son. Using simple tools, Egyptian goldsmiths fully mastered the techniques of casting, chasing, engraving, and embossing. They could draw gold into fine wires, hammer it into sheets for gilding furniture and weapons, or beat it—as they did for Tutankhamen—into splendid caskets and face masks. And they were so adept at soldering that, on gold settings of various jewels, the joints between the gold and soldering compounds are virtually undetectable.

Cutters of precious stone worked alongside the goldsmiths, as did glassmakers, who by Tutankhamen's reign were creating inlays that beautifully imitated the finest gemstones. In the same workshops there were joiners, cabinetmakers, and others who inlaid or covered their products with gold. Most of these artisans worked in complete anonymity; but a few received the ultimate honor of being portrayed in a patron's tomb.

Working with adze and chisel, wood-carvers prepare decorations to be used on a gilded shrine.

Seated at a charcoal-filled brazier, a smith soldering gold directs his flame with a blowpipe.

A goldsmith, using polished stone as a hammer, delicately chisels an asp on a sphinx's head.

official list of pharaohs: his name comes right after Amenhotep's, Akhenaten's father.

If Tutankhamen was Akhenaten's son, he certainly inherited none of his father's intellectual bent or his dedication to a lofty cause. He easily fell into the traditional ways pharaohs favored for passing the time, especially hunting. He had his artists render him bagging every kind of game from fowl to lions. One picture shows him in a chariot with bow and arrow, running down ostriches. It appears on a fan whose feathers, an inscription explains, came from an ostrich he had shot himself.

In another picture the scene is a rectangular pool set in a lush bower. Tutankhamen is seated to one side on a cushioned chair, his feet on a footstool, his adoring wife squatting beside him. He is launching an arrow at an unwary duck flapping about—not quite shooting sitting ducks, but not far from it. In yet another picture, decorating one side of a casket, he is back in his chariot firing arrows at a pride of lions, each and every shaft reaching its mark causing a leonine massacre. However, since another face of the same casket shows him in the chariot slaughtering an army of Syrians with the same success, and since he probably never left the borders of Egypt, much less faced an enemy army, the lion-shooting may have as little to do with reality as the idyllic bird-shooting in the bower.

The young couple had no surviving children. Two babies were stillborn; their remains were found in Tutankhamen's tomb encased in a pair of miniature coffins. His wife lived on after him, a widow anxious to remarry. In the decade before World War I archaeologists uncovered a mass of documents belonging to the official archives of the Hittites, an Asia Minor people who, just about Tutankhamen's time, became one of the ranking nations of the Near East. One document tells of an Egyptian queen—unnamed, but she can only be Ankhesenamen—who writes to the Hittite king as follows: "My husband died and I have no son. People say that you have many sons. If you were to send me one of your sons, he might become my husband."

Since Egyptian royal ladies did not normally look for mates from outside their own borders, the king suspected a trick and in his reply said as much. In high dudgeon the queen answers: "Why do you say ... 'Try to deceive' ... ? If I had a son, would I write to a foreign country in a manner which is humiliating to myself and to my country? ... He who was my husband died and I have no sons. Shall I perhaps take one of my servants and make him my husband? I have not written to any other country, I have written [only] to you." This time the Hittite king was convinced and sent one of his sons. As luck would have it, the groom-to-be was assassinated en route. Another Hittite document reports—as one might have anticipated—that the incident provoked hostilities, but no more is heard of Ankhesenamen.

Tutankhamen himself died unexpectedly. This is clear from the way he was buried—hastily and in a makeshift tomb, since his own was not ready. The switch to a new burial chamber was the first in a chain of fortuitous circumstances that combined to preserve his treasure for discovery. Had he been laid away where he should have been, robbers might very well have cleaned out his resting place as thoroughly as they had all the others. The tomb he was found in, with only four small chambers, was certainly not intended for a full-fledged member of the royal family. There are distinct signs that things were done in a hurry. The body of the great stone outer coffin and its lid are not mates: the body is of sandstone, the lid of granite. What is more, the workmen cracked the lid—it weighs close to two tons, and they were operating with the most primitive means possible. But they put the lid on just as it was, crack and all.

Actually robbers had managed to get into the tomb at least twice. But the break-ins must have occurred shortly after the burial, and the felons must have been caught or scared away because they made off with little. The first time they were after gold and went about snapping gold fittings off pieces of furniture and rummaging in caskets. The second time they were after the costly oils and unguents stored in alabaster vessels. Both times

Wearing robes pleated in the Egyptian fashion, emissaries from Nubia bear tribute for Tutankhamen, including oxen, rings of gold, and a giraffe. This scene is from the tomb of Huy, Tut's viceroy in Nubia, who greatly enriched the pharaoh's treasury.

the authorities, working at top speed, put things back into place as best they could and closed up the entrance—leaving their seals on the door each time.

Then came the vital stroke of good fortune. Two hundred years later, Ramses VI elected to have his tomb hacked out of the rock just above Tutankhamen's. Masses of rubble extracted by his workmen were dumped in front of Tutankhamen's door, burying it deeply. From that moment on, there was scant chance that robbers would find the tomb.

Thirty-two centuries after the eighteen-year-old Tutankhamen died, an eighteen-year-old Englishman, Howard Carter, joined Sir Flinders Petrie to excavate the very city where the young king had lived before taking over the throne. Sir Flinders was famous, but Carter's name was then as obscure as Tutankhamen's was.

By the eve of World War I, archaeologists had gone through the Valley of the Kings so thoroughly that they had found just about every pharaoh buried there. One was missing: a little-known figure, Tutankhamen. Carter's single-minded ambition was to discover his tomb. He managed to enlist the backing of a wealthy fellow countryman, the earl of Carnarvon.

They began work in 1917. For five arduous years they dug and dug without coming across a single object of importance, to say nothing of the tomb of Tutankhamen. The work went painfully slowly. The only way to haul dirt and rubble in those days was by filling up baskets and having porters cart them off. In this primitive fashion they moved an estimated 200,000 tons.

By the summer of 1922, Lord Carnarvon was ready to give up. Carter begged for a last effort: there was one small area at the foot of the approach to the tomb of Ramses VI that they had deliberately skipped their first season in order not to block tourists' access to that very popular sight. Carter asked for one more campaign to dig out that area. He offered, if it yielded nothing, to pay the costs out of his own pocket. Lord Carnarvon told him to go ahead on the old basis.

Divinities launch Tutankhamen on his voyage to the afterlife in this wall painting from the king's tomb. At top, twin images of the underworld god Osiris aboard a solar vessel worship a scarab, symbol of both the sun and life. The baboons below evoke the hours of the night.

Carter left England and began his all-or-nothing season of excavation on November 1, 1922. Three days later his men came upon a step cut in solid stone and, on the next day, eleven more. At the end of these they could see the top of a doorway which could open only into a tunnel in the rock—and which bore the seal of the ancient cemetery authorities. Carter fired off a cable to his patron. It was the one promising strike they had made in six years, and if anything was to be found, Carter wanted him to share the experience.

On November 24 Lord Carnarvon, his daughter, and Carter stood before the door, now totally cleared. Upon it were seals of Tutankhamen, but also the later seals of the cemetery authorities. They had been inside after the king was buried and then had resealed the tomb. In antiquity, obviously, there had been a robbery. The question of questions was: how much had the thieves made away with? The answer is now history.

The purely monetary value of the objects found in Tutankhamen's tomb is so staggering as to overshadow yet another value they possess in equal measure: they are artistic as well as material treasures—the products of gifted sculptors, painters, and craftsmen. What is more, they reveal that, though the Amarna age had come to an end politically, it had not ended artistically, at least not completely. Some of the things buried with the young king show unmistakable signs of the Amarna style. The figures tend toward the heavy, rounded buttocks and slender legs that were de rigueur in Akhenaten's lifetime. The king and queen are portrayed in intimate moments—not as intimate as Akhenaten and Nefertiti, but more so than tradition dictated. In the picture of Tutankhamen smiting the Syrian army, the faces of the wounded express pain—a touch of naturalism found only in Amarna art.

The furnishings of the young pharaoh's tomb are the greatest treasure trove to emerge so far from the ancient world—extraordinary in themselves and tantalizing in their implications about the treasures that have vanished.

A BOY-KING'S GOLDEN TROVE

Two figures of Tutankhamen, inlaid with colored glass, face each other on this gold unguent case. The black head of the left-hand figure probably symbolizes rebirth.

To help render Tutankhamen incorruptible after death, the prime material for his burial treasure was divine, imperishable gold—more than two tons of it. During the seventy-day embalming ritual, royal artisans labored frantically to complete the trappings for his funeral. Then a great procession of mourners, led by priests and nobles, bore the mummy on a canopied sledge across the Nile and on to the tomb entrance. Because the king died prematurely, his grave consisted of a small four-room sepulcher hastily built amid the vast resting places of earlier pharaohs in the Valley of the Kings, opposite Thebes. But into this modest space went an extraordinary wealth of objects that, like those here and on the following pages, attest to the exalted status of even this young and relatively powerless pharaoh.

The greatest wealth was placed in the burial chamber itself. At the center lay the king, swathed in yards of fine linen that held 143 personal ornaments, from gold finger sheaths to breast-wide pendants. A gold mask covered his face. And enclosing the mummy were a series of ornate cases, one fitted inside the other like Chinese boxes: first, three inlaid coffins, the innermost of solid gold; then a massive stone sarcophagus; and finally four outer casings of magnificently gilded wood.

Among the pieces in adjoining rooms were belongings from the palace, such as furniture and clothes, that Tutankhamen had enjoyed in life and would enjoy again in the hereafter. Other objects had been created as splendid tomb gifts. Elaborately decorated, often with figures of deities in the guise of animals, they would ensure the king's rebirth and safe passage through the netherworld. Aided by these treasures, and safe in his luxurious nest of gold, Tutankhamen, the "son of the Sun," was at last ready to make his way to eternity.

Nearly eight feet across, this shrine, at left, from Tutankhamen's burial chamber is made of oak covered with burnished leaves of gold foil. The entire surface bears embossed scenes and sacred texts relating stages in the king's afterlife.

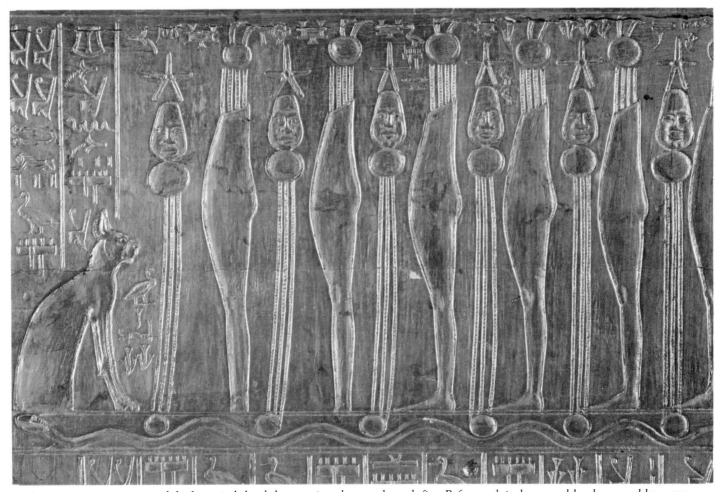

In this enigmatic scene, a cat, left, faces six beheaded mummies whose necks gush fire. Before each is the severed head crowned by a star.

Nephthys, opposite, a goddess of the netherworld, waves her wings to move air over Tutankhamen's soul on this panel detail from one of the dead pharaoh's gilded shrines. The goddess is standing on the symbol for gold, and inscribed around her are spells she utters promising the young king everlasting life. "I have come to protect thee," she tells him. "Thou shalt not decay."

OVERLEAF: On the shrine doors, deities welcome Tutankhamen into the netherworld. On the left door, the king—at center, wearing a double crown—faces Osiris, lord of eternity, who grants that he will be a "living god." Reaching out behind Tutankhamen is the goddess Isis. On the right door, the king is flanked by the falcon-headed god Re-Harakhti, at left, and Maat, goddess of truth.

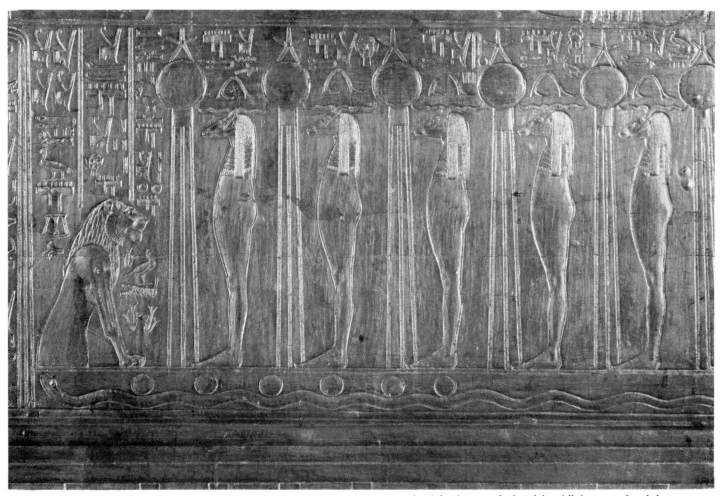

A lion, its hindquarters buried, faces a row of ram-headed mummies; between each of the figures, shafts of fire fall from a solar disk.

In this central detail from the burial shrine, the mummy of Tutankhamen, now in the netherworld, stands with head and feet encircled by two serpents biting their tails. At the center of the mummy is a disk with a ram-headed bird inside, symbolizing the night sun. To the left, figures with raised arms pull the disk with a rope, probably to signal the passing of the night.

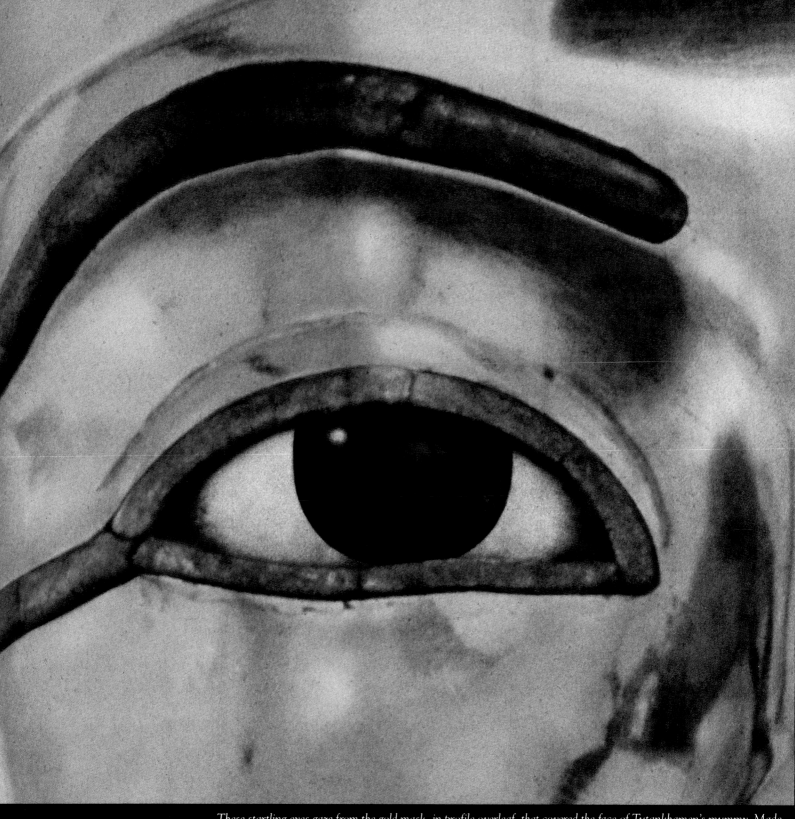

These startling eyes gaze from the gold mask, in profile overleaf, that covered the face of Tutankhamen's mummy. Made

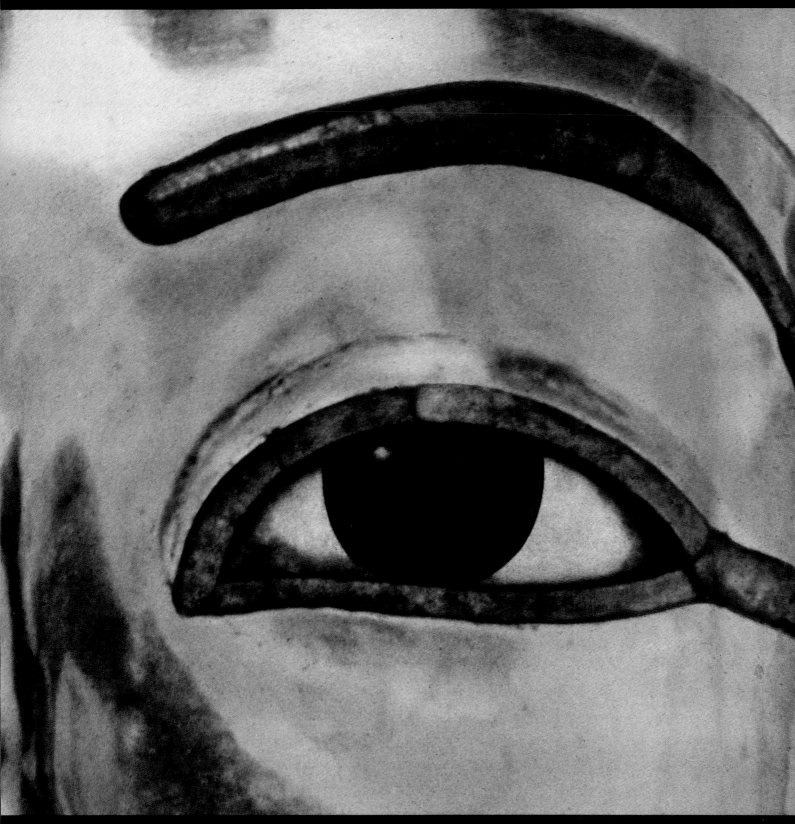

of quartz and obsidian and accented at the sides with strips of lapis lazuli, they also symbolize the sun and moon.

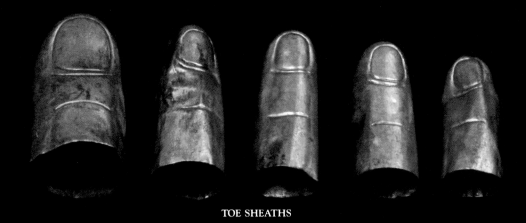

TOE SHEATHS

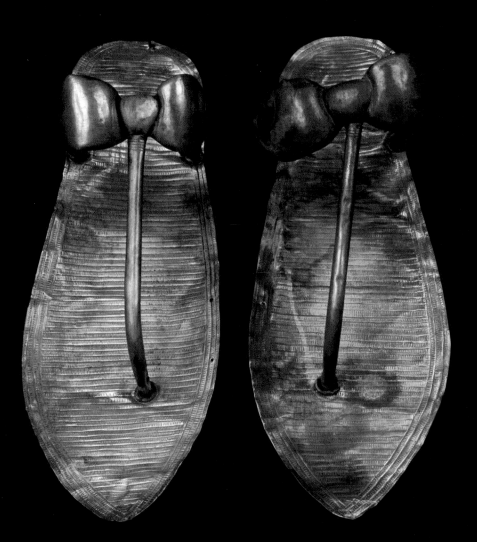

TUTANKHAMEN'S GOLD SANDALS

Gold completely encased the head and extremities of the young pharaoh's mummy, identifying him with the powerful sun god Re, whose flesh was of gold. Upon Tutankhamen's shoulders sat the majestic gold mask, in profile opposite, which has a headdress inlaid with stripes of blue glass and a wide collar encrusted with semiprecious stones. The finely modeled ears are pierced for earrings, and the brow bears a vulture and cobra, representing the two divinities of Upper and Lower Egypt. The beard, also inlaid with blue glass, likens the king to the underworld god Osiris. The gold sheaths, above, capped his toes, and he wore similar ones on his fingers. The pair of sandals at left, their insoles delicately ribbed, covered the royal feet.

THE GOLD BURIAL MASK

This vulture's head and cobra, symbols of Tutankhamen's sovereignty over Upper and Lower
Egypt, adorn the headband—in detail here—of a
gold diadem. The band, which is also decorated
with carnelian roundels and gold bosses, encircled
the king's head beneath his gold mask. The vulture
and cobra are detachable; at his burial they were
disassembled and placed over each thigh. During his
reign, however, the king very likely wore the as-
sembled diadem over a wig. The wavy band arching
behind the cobra is its tail, which helped hold the
royal headpiece in place.

Queen Ankhesenamen reaches out to anoint Tutankhamen in this splendid scene on the back of a gilded throne, which was probably made for the king's coronation. The elegant figures, both wearing elaborate headdresses and necklaces, are inlaid with colored glass and semiprecious stones; their robes are made of silver. An artist trained at Amarna must have executed the work, for it has the intimate, relaxed style of Amarna art. Above the royal pair shines the sun disk worshiped by Akhenaten, its gold rays ending in life-giving hands.

Clusters of finely granulated gold balls and bands inlaid with gemstone and colored glass decorate this hilt of the superb gold dagger on the opposite page. The inlay work appears to be true cloisonné, meaning that the gems and glass were fired in place like enamel. Even more elaborate is the sheath, shown on both sides in this montage. The side above the dagger is almost entirely covered with a minute feather pattern in red and blue cloisonné. The reverse bears an exquisite scene, embossed in high relief, of a lion, leopard, and hound—symbolic animals considered friendly to man—attacking their prey.

One of the most elegant, and mysterious, of *Tutankhamen's* treasures is this model ship, carved from alabaster and set atop a pedestal in a painted alabaster tank. Both bow and stern end in the finely sculpted head of an ibex capped with real horns. What seems to be an open sarcophagus sits under a canopy amidships. Behind the prow, a seated woman clasps an ivory lotus to her chest, while a dwarf near the stern poles the vessel. The work of a highly imaginative artist, the structure may have been a special container for unguents or simply a dazzling palace ornament.

Two Nile deities decorate an alabaster perfume vase and attached stand, which bears falcons flanking the king's cartouche. Nearly twenty-eight inches high, it is embellished with gold and painted ivory.

The figure of Shu, god of the air, forms the center-piece of this headrest, made from two pieces of carved ivory joined by a wooden dowel and gold nails. According to legend, Shu brought chaos to an end by holding the sky—represented by the curved head support—high above the earth. The two lions at the base symbolize mountains at the eastern and western horizons, marking the path of the sun. To the Egyptians the head was the seat of life. Lifted upward at death, it would slowly rise to heaven and acknowledge its own rebirth.

131

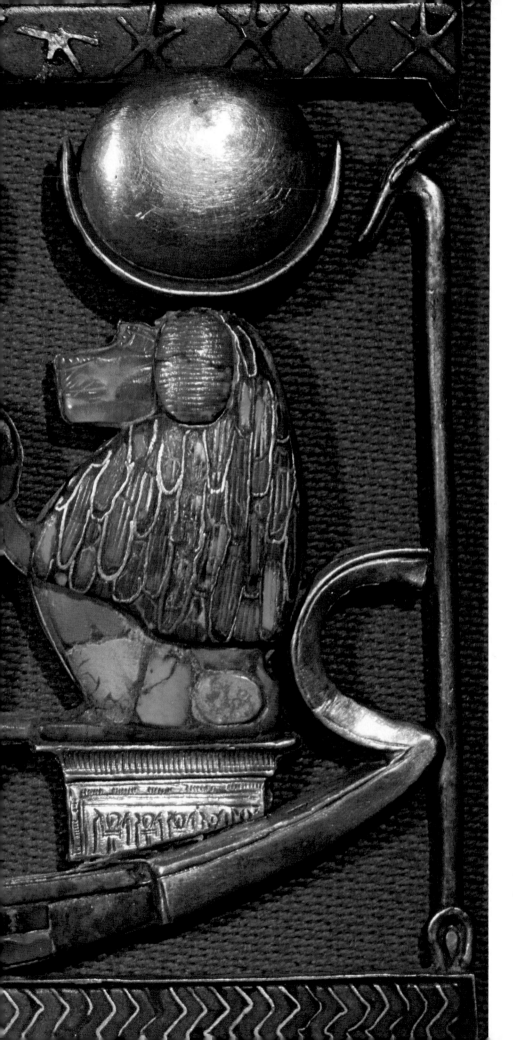

The rising of the sun—a favorite theme during the reign of Tutankhamen—is the motif on this sparkling pendant wrought from gold and semiprecious stones. A scarab beetle of deep blue lapis lazuli, representing the sun god at dawn, elevates a solar disk carved from carnelian. Worshiping him on either side are two baboons, each with a crescent and disk of the moon above its head. All three figures sit inside a celestial boat, which carried the sun and moon on their journeys across the firmament. Above and below the figures are strips of lapis lazuli inlaid with gold, signifying the sky and sea.

Suspended from the neck of Tutankhamen's mummy, this solid-gold necklace, its pendant shaped like a vulture, lay within the innermost wrappings that contained personal possessions the king had used in his lifetime. Representing the vulture goddess Nekhbet, patron deity of Upper Egypt, the pendant is attached to straps of gold and lapis lazuli that end in a clasp, below, of two nesting falcons. The hammered details of the gold are masterful, with the wings beautifully feathered and fine wrinkles covering the back of the vulture's head. Its talons clutch the Egyptian sign for infinity, and as a royal attribute, the bird wears a miniature pendant under its neck inscribed with Tutankhamen's cartouche.

A vulture and cobra protect the wadjet eye—a symbol for health—on this pendant hanging from a necklace of faience and gold.

Fringed on the bottom with glass flowers, the ornate pendant opposite glitters with a multitude of lunar and solar symbols. At the center is an exquisitely carved chalcedony scarab with the extremities of a falcon—a dual symbol of the sun god. On the silver disk at top, above a celestial boat holding a sacred eye, the moon god Thoth and sun god Re flank the figure of the king.

OVERLEAF: *The most elaborate of Tutankhamen's amulets is this great collar in the form of the goddess Nekhbet. The shimmering wings, draped over the king's chest, are composed of 250 separate gold plaques inlaid with feathers of colored glass that imitates turquoise, jasper, and lapis lazuli. The collar is flexible, each plaque linked to the others by thread passing through tiny gold eyelets.*

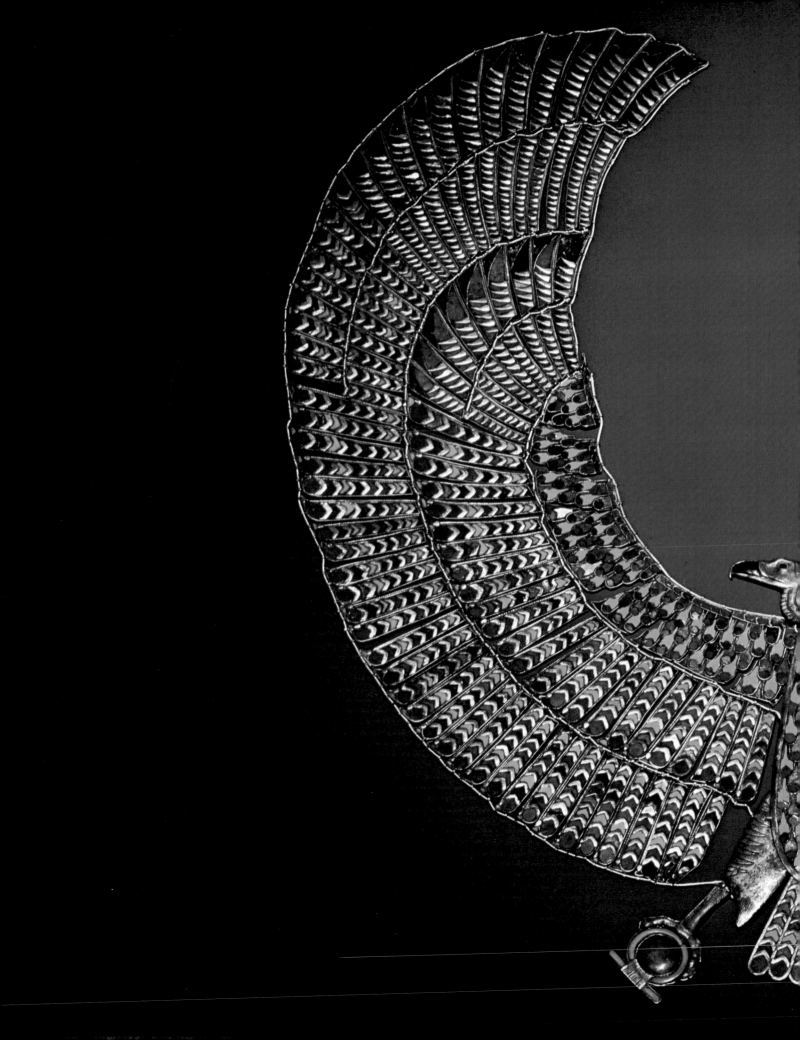

V

A LEGACY OF RUINS

RAMSES THE GREAT

Egypt had lost much ground, both domestically and internationally, during Akhenaten's troubled years. The great heretic had been too busy with religion to bother much with affairs of state: local administration became sloppy, and Palestine was able to slip out of Egypt's control. And Tutankhamen and his mentors were too busy undoing what Akhenaten had done to take any steps forward. But when Haremhab grasped the reins, Egypt started on the road to recovery. He held the throne for almost thirty years, a long rule that seems to have been both just and efficient.

Haremhab was followed by Ramses I and Seti I, father and son, who initiated a new dynasty, the Nineteenth. They brought the country much further along—particularly Seti; a warrior in the style of Thutmose III, he led Egypt's soldiers back through Palestine to the borders of Syria. When he died he handed over a strong and wealthy nation to his own son, the second Ramses.

Ramses II, a young man with sixty-five years of rule still ahead

Ramses II brandishes a mace to smite a group of Asiatic captives in this temple relief, one of many the pharaoh commissioned to glorify his might in battle.

A headdress encircled by sacred cobras crowns the figure of Queen Tuy, mother of Ramses II. The queen holds a lily scepter in her left hand, and in her right, the remnant of a crook—regalia of her authority over Upper and Lower Egypt.

of him in which to make his mark, was so effective that his influence is still to be seen the length and breadth of the land. A number of pharaohs were prodigious builders; Ramses outdid them all. His taste ran to outsized creations—the hypostyle hall at Karnak, the Ramesseum across the river from it, the temple of Abu Simbel far below the First Cataract. In fact, almost half the temples whose ruins stand today were raised at his command. Others he cavalierly took credit for by striking out the name of the pharaoh who had actually put them up and substituting his own. And wherever he could he garnished with gargantuan statues of himself, such as the one that provided the inspiration for the great English poet Shelley's "Ozymandias." Ozymandias was the pronounciation given in Shelley's day to User-maat-re, another of Ramses' names. The poem describes a colossal stone figure that has been broken and decapitated, the head shattered and half buried in the sand,

> *And on the pedestal these words appear:*
> *"My name is Ozymandias, king of kings:*
> *Look on my works, ye Mighty, and despair!"*

Such ambitious projects as Ramses' took an enormous amount of labor to carry out. His solution, at least in certain places, was to conscript Jews. For, in the opinion of most authorities, Ramses was the pharaoh of the Exodus.

The forced labor of prisoners of war was not uncommon in Egypt during the centuries when bellicose pharaohs, such as Thutmose III or Amenhotep II, ruled the land; they would storm up into Palestine or down into Nubia and come back with hordes of captives. Many of these were promptly enrolled in the Egyptian armed forces, but some entered the work gangs assigned to the estates belonging to temples, or quarries.

According to the account in the Old Testament, there had been Jews in Egypt ever since the time of Joseph, that is, probably since the flourishing period of the Eighteenth Dynasty, about 1560 B.C. According to the Biblical account, Joseph was sold into slavery by his brothers to some passing merchants. Later, wealthy and powerful, he welcomed his impoverished family into Egypt. During hard times in Canaan, the Jews (as well as other peoples) no doubt migrated into Egypt. They seem to have continued on as a welcome element in the population long after Joseph died, until there "arose up a new king over Egypt, which knew not Joseph"—presumably Ramses II—who introduced the policy that brought upon them "taskmasters to afflict them with their burdens."

Egyptian chronicles never mention this, but that is hardly surprising. Their public documents concentrate on how the pharaoh destroyed his enemies, not staffed his work gangs. In any case, the conscripts worked in the delta area, where the rainy climate rules out the survival of private documents, which were written on papyrus. The earliest incontrovertible reference to Jews does not occur until the reign of Ramses' successor Merneptah (1224–1214 B.C.). In an inscription Merneptah boasts of all the foes he has wiped out, asserting that, "Israel is laid low, his seed is not."

But there are earlier, if less certain references to the Jews. Documents from the time of Thutmose III and later frequently mention a people from Palestine whose name is spelled Apiru or Habiru. Many experts claim that these are none other than the Hebrews. They figure among the enemies the pharaoh's armies faced in and around Palestine, and Egypt's victories resulted in the capture of numbers of them. In 1444 B.C., when Amenhotep II marched up to the Sea of Galilee, he returned, he claimed, with 3,600 Apiru prisoners of war. Others could well have been captured by Ramses' hard-fighting father or Ramses himself.

According to the Book of Exodus, the Israelites "built for Pharaoh treasure cities, Pithom and Raamses." Pithom was a town in the Wadi Tumilat, the fertile depression that runs due east from the Nile through the desert east of the delta to Ismailia at the southern end of the Suez Canal. Raamses, also known as Pi-Rameses, was the name Ramses II gave to a town just north of

Sucking on his finger, Ramses II as a child sits protected by the falcon Horus, god of the sky. The statue bears symbols forming the pharaoh's name: Re, the sun disk above his head; mes, the child; and sou, the sedge plant in his left hand.

GUIDEBOOK FOR THE AFTERLIFE

All Egyptians in New Kingdom times expected a life beyond the grave. But to gain entree, they believed that every person, after death, had to stand in judgment before Osiris, god of the underworld. Seated on a throne, Osiris would look on, as his assistant Anubis, a jackal-headed deity, operated a set of scales. On one side he placed the deceased's heart, which contained the mind and soul. Occupying the other side was the symbol for *ma'at*, or truth, usually an ostrich feather. Apparently the heart and feather were meant to balance for a favorable judgment. Should the soul be found unworthy, a fierce beast stood nearby, ready to destroy the mummy's heart.

To contend with this and other postmortem trials, the Egyptians devised a complex system of spells, prayers, and liturgies that were recorded on papyrus and placed in the tomb. A key passage in the Book of the Dead—the modern title for any of various versions of these texts—listed thirty-six denials of sin to recite, beginning with "I have not committed evil against men." Another pleaded, "Oh my heart ... speak not against me in the presence of the judges." Such appeals presumably assured a benign verdict when facing Osiris and his assessors.

Use of the Book of the Dead, which had been proscribed by the heretical pharaoh Akhenaten, greatly expanded under Ramses II and his successors. Copies would often be embellished with vignettes like the one at right, taken from the papyrus entombed with a Ramesside scribe. Such artistry was strictly practical. Like the text, it guided and protected the deceased, enabling him to merge with Osiris and begin a renewed life in the hereafter.

Anubis weighs the heart of a mummy against a feather representing truth. If the scales do not balance, the

heart will be thrown to the monster waiting at far right.

Pithom that had previously been called Tanis. His predecessors in the Nineteenth Dynasty, giving up Thebes, had made it their capital. Ramses renamed it after himself and, just as the Old Testament records, undertook an ambitious building program.

Ramses was not content to let buildings and statues alone tell the tale of his greatness. He larded them with inscriptions that spelled it out, that testified to his prowess in all areas, from the harem (one inscription names over a hundred of his sons and daughters) to the battlefield. His mortal enemies were the Hittites, ever since Tutankhamen's day Egypt's most powerful neighbor and her rival for control of Palestine. Ramses trumpets the beatings he adminstered to them, boasts of how they obsequiously sought his favor with gifts that included not only "gold, silver . . . horses without limit . . . cattle, goats, and sheep by the ten-thousands," but even the king's eldest daughter. "She was fair of face like a goddess . . . beautiful in the heart of His Majesty, and he loved her more than anything."

Today Egyptologists, with the light of history to help them, view his reign with a harder eye. The victories over the Hittites that he touted were pure bombast. He managed to fight nothing better than staying actions and willingly signed a treaty whose terms make it clear that neither side had beaten the other. And if he was indeed the pharaoh of the Exodus, he suffered the ignominy of seeing a part of the population he had oppressed safely elude his grasp and escape into the Sinai desert.

His building was as showy and insubstantial as his military triumphs. The celebrated hall at Karnak is a prime example. A forest of mammoth columns reduces all who enter into mere pygmies. Yet they are set on poor and ill-prepared foundations and covered with hasty and mediocre carving. The equally celebrated temple at Abu Simbel, cut into a cliff along the Nile, has one of the most impressive entrances ever designed, a portal flanked on either side by a pair of Brobdingnagian statues of Ramses hewn out of the solid rock. The portal is pure show: it leads into nothing more than a couple of low, modest rooms.

TEXT CONTINUED ON PAGE 152

For amusement in her afterlife, Nefertari reaches out to play senet, a board game with pieces like chess. In her right hand, she holds a scepter.

HOMAGE TO A BEAUTIFUL COMPANION

Ramses II's consort and favorite queen was Nefertari, who probably married him before he became pharaoh. She managed to retain his affections even though he had four other wives and countless concubines. Indeed, her name means "the most beautiful of them," and Ramses commemorated his love for her on many stone monuments. The finest tribute she received was in her tomb at Thebes in the Valley of the Queens. Its construction was typical—a long passageway, dug in limestone, that led to a small chamber containing the sarcophagus. Adorning every wall were painted reliefs that

are among the finest in the tombs at Thebes.

Because the limestone was of inferior quality, sculptors coated the walls with a thick layer of plaster into which they cut their reliefs. This new technique yielded unusually bold outlines for the figures, which artists then painted in blazing colors. Most of these murals, in detail here and on pages 148–151, portray Nefertari on her journey through the underworld, surrounded by various deities and writings from the Book of the Dead. Dressed in linen gowns and jeweled headdresses, she enters eternity looking as splendid as she no doubt did in life.

A goddess, whose outstretched arms support wings, kneels above the doorway leading from the corridor into the sarcophagus chamber of Nefertari's tomb. Inscribed along the sides of the doorway are the queen's name and titles, proclaiming her as the "Great King's wife, Lady of Two Lands," Lower and Upper Egypt.

Deities and sacred texts, all brightly limned, line a section of the corridor and recess leading to a side room in Nefertari's tomb. Two gods of the underworld adorn the outermost walls: Osiris, in the form of a mummy, is at far left and jackal-headed Anubis on the right. The lintel above the recess bears a frieze of cobras flanking a kneeling figure. Three deities sit enthroned on the inner wall by the doorway. The god at left has a beetle for his face, a sign identifying him with the sun. The pair to the right—a female in an ornamented gown reaching out to her falcon-headed partner—wait to receive Nefertari, whose figure, not visible in this view, is on an adjoining wall.

Nefertari stands before Thoth, an ibis-headed god who was the patron of scribes and writing, in this vignette from the Book of the Dead. The accompanying text, inscribed on the left half of the wall, is a spell asking for the god's sacred writing palette.

Three deities—a ram-headed god, a goddess with a feline head topped by snakes, and a human figure—guard one of a series of gates and doors in the sarcophagus chamber, the final point in Nefertari's journey. By passing through these portals, her soul leaves the world of the tomb to at last enter the domain of Osiris.

TEXT CONTINUED FROM PAGE 145

The Book of Exodus describes Ramses' capital as a "treasure city." He must have been as lavish with precious metals and gems to testify to his wealth as he was with buildings to testify to his might and inscriptions to his valor in war. He himself was buried at Thebes, where his tomb and mummy were stripped by robbers as thoroughly as all the others. Whatever he may have had on display at Tanis has vanished without trace. The only treasure found there was a handful of tombs of some pharaohs who ruled two hundred years after Ramses' death. At this time Egypt had broken into two separate kingdoms, Upper and Lower Egypt, and the pharaohs at Tanis, ruling Lower Egypt and hence without access to Thebes, had themselves buried locally. The corpses were adorned with rich, finely fashioned jewelry. If such wealth went into the graves of the likes of these feeble and obscure monarchs, the thought of what must have gone into Ramses' boggles the imagination.

His successors were to preside over Egypt's long decline. "The foreign countries made a conspiracy in their islands [presumably the islands of the eastern Mediterranean]...No land could stand before their arms...A camp was set up in one place in Amor [Syria]. They desolated its people, and its land was like that which has never come into being. They were coming forward toward Egypt, while the flame was prepared before them."

So reads an inscription of Ramses III, who ruled two decades after the death of Ramses II, from 1194 to 1163. Egypt saved herself, but the effort left her exhausted. Giving up her extraterritorial possessions to both north and south, she shrank back, as in the long-ago days of the Old Kingdom, into the embrace of the valley of the Nile. A century later even this area could no longer hold together, which was when the two separate Egypts came into being.

Adversity knocked the cockiness and gaiety out of the Egyptian character. The change can be seen clearly in the

Ramses II lassos a bull, as his son holds it by the tail, in a rite pictured in a carving on a temple wall. Bulls symbolized strength: after being captured and slaughtered at royal rodeos, their flesh was consumed by nobles and offered to the gods.

pictures and texts they now put on the walls of their tombs. The pictures no longer portray the serene scenes of life on earth that the deceased will reenjoy in the hereafter but rather the fearsome new experiences that await him—judgment before the gods of the underworld, and meetings with strange and terrible demons. The texts are no longer boastful bits of autobiography but long religious screeds whose purpose is to supply magical protection. In this age Egyptian religion changes radically, becoming more and more a set of superstitious practices. What counts now is the scrupulously proper performance of a ritual, the verbatim repetition of prayers and formulas. These, along with witchcraft, magic, and demonology, take the place of meaningful worship.

Around 720 B.C., Egypt suffered what she had been spared ever since the departure of the Hyksos—invasion by foreigners. The first to take over the country were the Sudanese marching up from the south. In a way, they were not too bad. They had been Egyptianized for centuries, so their rule marked no real break; things went on in the wonted Egyptian fashion.

But the same could hardly be said of the next wave of invaders. In the first half of the seventh century B.C. the merciless Assyrians descended irresistibly upon Egypt as they had upon the rest of the Near East. They were followed by the Persians, who ruled with some interruptions to 332 B.C.—the year Alexander the Great stormed into Egypt, took it away from them, and set his mark upon it by founding Alexandria.

Alexander's entry heralds Egypt's rebirth as a ranking nation, no longer under its own rulers but under pharaohs of Greek descent. In the dividing up of Alexander's conquered territories after his death, Ptolemy Soter, one of his most able generals, snatched Egypt for himself. He made Alexandria his capital, building it up into the architectural and cultural center of the Mediterranean world. For this, and for an army and navy, he needed money—lots of it. In Egypt, that was no problem.

The fertile soil, refreshed and watered by the annual flood of the Nile, guaranteed grain in quantity, and in those times grain

A female acrobat, wearing only a kilt and earrings, sweeps the ground with her hair as she performs a backward somersault. During the Nineteenth Dynasty, acrobats as well as musicians and dancers provided the chief amusements at royal banquets.

commanded the market that oil does today. As a Greek savant observed: "The Nile is the one river that can truly be called 'gold-flowing'; with the boundless crops [it nurtures], it brings down pure gold." Ptolemy and his successors, running the country with flint-hearted efficiency, amassed riches that may have surpassed those of even a Thutmose or a Ramses. Here, for example, is a contemporary description of some of the precious objects to be seen in a lavish procession put on by the second Ptolemy (282–246 B.C.):

In the procession were 350 golden censers, also gilded altars wreathed with crowns of gold; on one altar were fastened four 15-foot golden torches ... There were nine golden tripods six feet high, another eight that were nine feet high, and one that was forty-five feet high and was topped by seven-and-a-half-foot golden statues...There were 3,200 wreaths of gold in the procession, including one, studded with gems, that was 120 feet in circumference.

And all this was only a fraction of the whole. The account goes on to tell of four hundred cartloads of silver vessels, twenty of gold vessels, innumerable suits of gold armor, and much more.

The Ptolemies ruled Egypt for three hundred years until, like the rest of the lands around the Mediterranean, it was swallowed up in the Roman Empire.

For the next six centuries Nile grain and Nubian gold flowed first to Rome and then to Constantinople. In A.D. 642 the Arabs, in the full tide of the great movement that carried Islam far and wide, annexed Egypt, and the flow shifted to Mecca, Damascus, Baghdad. The Arabs were masters in Egypt for nine centuries, ample time to implant Arab culture deeply. Then came the Turks and finally the British. Not until the middle of this century did Egypt regain her independence—independence, but not treasure. For the Nile is no longer "gold-flowing." It nurtures cotton today instead of grain, and cotton is hardly as important now as grain was to the ancient world. Oil is what the modern world craves. And so it is Arab sheikhs who boast the kind of wealth that once the pharaohs boasted.

A MASSIVE
STONE LEGACY

Two solemn faces of Ramses II, carved side by side from living rock, face the rising sun on the facade of the pharaoh's temple at Abu Simbel.

R amses II, ruling over ancient Egypt during
its last prolonged period of peace, undertook a building program that was one of the
most ambitious the world has ever known. Over
a span of nearly forty years, beginning about
1260 B.C., the vainglorious king erected scores
of statues, temples, and obelisks throughout
Upper and Lower Egypt. The sites that pro-
claim his greatness include the capital at
Thebes—modern Karnak and Luxor—where
he added grandiose monuments in a bid to out-
shine the works of earlier pharaohs. Two of his
most impressive temples, created for himself
and his wife Nefertari, sit in splendid isolation
far up the Nile at Abu Simbel.

To accomplish these feats of construction,
Ramses had a vast army of laborers directed by a
superb corps of masons and engineers. The
masons hewed out immense blocks of granite or
sandstone from the living rock—most likely by
hammering in wooden wedges that were then
soaked in water, causing them to expand and
split the rock along a chosen line. Once the
monument had been carved, workers using
wooden sleds and rollers transported it from the
quarry to the river, and loaded it onto a barge.
At the prepared site came the Herculean task of
raising the structure, probably carried out with
the aid of ramps and ropes.

Whatever he built, Ramses' taste almost in-
variably placed pride in size, rather than in
grace or elegance. In architectural conception,
his monuments lack any subtlety, and their interiors are never as imposing as the outside. But
the scale of his masterworks, like those here
and in detail on the following pages, is over-
whelming even today. The facades also possess
great dignity, a serene grandeur that achieves
what Ramses desired—to seize the minds of
men and establish his claim to immortality.

*Cut into sandstone bluffs above the Nile, four
seated statues of Ramses II flank the entrance to
the Great Temple at Abu Simbel. Each of the
figures is sixty-five feet tall and weighs twelve
hundred tons. Smaller statues of some of the
royal family repose between the legs of the co-
lossuses, while an image of the sky god Re-Harakhti looks out from a recess above the doorway.*

157

Eight stone effigies of Ramses II, all deified with features of the underworld lord Osiris, guard a sanctuary 180 feet within the temple.

Above the figures of Ramses, painted vultures with outspread wings cover the temple ceiling at Abu Simbel like a great tapestry. The birds represent Nekhbet, goddess of Upper Egypt. Probably to exalt his thirty-year jubilee, which occurred on or near October 20, 1260 B.C., Ramses planned the temple so that sunlight shines directly into this innermost sanctuary only twice each year—in October and February.

Nefertari stands between statues of Ramses on the facade of her temple. Separating the figures are inscribed buttresses.

This imposing figure of Nefertari, her breasts showing beneath a wig, hugs the leg of one of the great statues of Ramses guarding the pharaoh's temple. Ramses also immortalized his consort with a separate temple (above), set several hundred feet north of his own at Abu Simbel.

This toppled head of Ramses II lies in ruined grandeur in the courtyard of his funerary temple at Thebes. The statue that it once crowned,

among the largest ever erected by the pharaoh, was hewn from a single block of granite and weighed more than one thousand tons.

A forest of columns in dusky sandstone form part of the hypostyle (meaning "pillared") hall, a building in the grand temple complex at Karnak dedicated to the sun god Amen. The awesome scale of the hall, which was a collaboration between Ramses II and his father, Seti I, placed it among the great architectural feats of antiquity. The structure comprises a total of 134 pillars that cover an area about the size of a football field. The columns at right, bordering a central aisle, rise nearly eighty feet and measure twelve feet in diameter. Surrounding them are seven rows of smaller columns, their capitals shaped and painted to simulate papyrus buds. The shafts bear hieroglyphs, figures of gods, and scenes from the lives of Seti and Ramses, all deeply inscribed in order to prevent later kings from usurping the structure.

Ram-headed sphinxes erected by Ramses II crouch in front of the temple at Karnak honoring Amen. Usually a sphinx bore a human head,

but the ram was the emblem of the sun god. Between the paws of each beast stands a figure probably representing the pharaoh.

OVERLEAF: *Shadows settle around the weathered features on a fallen head of Ramses the Great. In the background are other colossal statues that bear hieroglyphs of the king's names and titles.*

EGYPT: A CHRONOLOGY

EPOCH	PEOPLE AND EVENTS		ART AND ARCHITECTURE	
OLD KINGDOM 2700–2200 B.C.	c. 2700	Foundation of capital at Memphis		
	c. 2660	Djoser		
			c. 2650	Djoser's Step Pyramid at Sakkara
	c. 2620	Snefru		
			c. 2600	Hetepheres' gilded bedchamber
	c. 2596	Cheops		
	c. 2565	Khafre		
	c. 2500	Menkaure	c. 2550	The Great Pyramids and the Great Sphinx at Giza
	r. 2300–2210	Pepi II		
MIDDLE KINGDOM c. 2000–1800 B.C.	r. 1991–1962	Amenemhet I		
	c. 1990	Gold mines at Nubia discovered		
	r. 1971–1928	Senusret I		
	r. 1929–1895	Amenemhet II		
	r. 1897–1878	Senusret II		
	r. 1878–1843	Senusret III	c. 1860	Mereret's, Khnumet's, and Sit-Hathor-Yunet's gold jewelry inlaid with valuable stones
	r. 1842–1797	Amenemhet III		
	c. 1675	Hyksos invade Egypt	c. 1600	Queen Ahhotep's gold, lapis lazuli, and enamel jewelry
	c. 1580	Kamose attacks Hyksos in Middle Egypt		
NEW KINGDOM 1576–1069 B.C.	r. 1576–1551	Ahmose I		
	c. 1575	Ahmose I completes revolt against Hyksos		
	c. 1570	Thebes made capital of all Egypt		
	r. 1530–1517	Thutmose I		
	r. 1517–1504	Thutmose II	c. 1550–1300	Temples to Amen at Thebes
	c. 1510	Military campaigns in Nubia and Palestine		
	r. 1504–1483	Hatshepsut		
	c. 1500	Trading expedition to Punt	c. 1500	Tombs at Valley of the Kings Hatshepsut's mortuary temple at Deir al-Bahri
	r. 1504–1450	Thutmose III		
	c. 1450	Egypt's borders extended south to Fourth Cataract, north into Syria	c. 1460	Thutmose III's wives' silver, gold, and glass tableware

EPOCH	PEOPLE AND EVENTS	ART AND ARCHITECTURE
	r. 1452–1420 Amenhotep II	
	r. 1401–1363 Amenhotep III	
NEW KINGDOM (CONTINUED)	r. 1363–1347 Amenhotep IV	c. 1363 Amenhotep IV's temple to Aten at Karnak
	1363–1349 Queen Nefertiti	
		1360 ff. Amarna style of art
	1357 Akhetaten (Amarna) made capital; Amenhotep IV changes his name to Akhenaten; decrees Amen no longer supreme god	
	r. 1349–1347 Smenkhare	
	r. 1347–1338 Tutankhamen	
	c. 1347 Thebes restored as capital; Amen resumes status as supreme god	c. 1340 Tutankhamen's tomb
	r. 1338–1334 Ay	
	r. 1334–1306 Haremhab	
	r. 1306–1305 Ramses I	
	r. 1305–1290 Seti I	
	r. 1290–1224 Ramses II	
	c. 1280 Ramses II makes Raamses his capital	c. 1250 Hypostyle hall at Karnak; temples at Abu Simbel
		c. 1240 Nefertari's tomb in the Valley of the Queens
	r. 1224–1214 Merneptah	
	r. 1194–1163 Ramses III	
	c. 720 Sudanese invade Egypt	
	c. 680 Assyrians invade Egypt	
	c. 450 Persians invade Egypt	
	332 Alexander the Great conquers Egypt	
	331 Alexandria founded	
	r. 305–283 Ptolemy I	
	Alexandria becomes architectural and cultural center of the Mediterranean	
	r. 282–246 Ptolemy II	

ACKNOWLEDGMENTS & CREDITS

Sources for the pictures in this book are shown below.
Abbreviations:
ÄM—Ägyptisches Museum, Staatliche Museen
Preussischer Kulturbesitz, Berlin (west)
MMA—Metropolitan Museum of Art, N.Y.

We would like to thank the following for their assistance:
Deanna Cross, Photographic Services, MMA; Dr. Hans
Goedicke, Johns Hopkins University; Dr. Timothy Ken-
dall, Museum of Fine Arts, Boston; M. Ahm. Mohssen,
General Director, Egyptian Museum, Cairo; Robert Musac-
chio, Photographic Services, Brooklyn Museum; Christine
Young, Harmer Johnson Books Ltd., N.Y.

Maps by H. Shaw Borst
Endsheet design by Cockerell Bindery/TALAS

Cover: Michael Jacobs/Woodfin Camp & Associates. 2:
Farrell Grehan/Photo Researchers. 4, 5: Erich Lessing/
Magnum. 6: MMA. 10: Jean Mazenod/Éditions d'Art Lu-
cien Mazenod. 12, 13: James Whitmore/Time Inc. 14: Brian
Brake/Photo Researchers. 15: Oriental Institute, University
of Chicago. 16, 17: George Holton/Photo Researchers. 18,
19: John G. Ross/Thames and Hudson Ltd. 20: Giraudon.
21: MMA. 22, 23: Rudolph Robinson/Museum of Fine
Arts, Boston. 24: John G. Ross, Rome. 25: Albert
Shoucair/Thames and Hudson Ltd. 26, 27: Skira S.A.
28-31: Albert Shoucair/Thames and Hudson Ltd. 32: Skira
S.A. 33: Kodansha Ltd. 34-40: MMA. 42-44: Erich Less-
ing/Magnum. 45: John G. Ross, Rome. 46, 47: Michael
Holford. 48: Brian Brake/Photo Researchers. 49: René Ro-
land/Ziolo. 50, 51: Albert Shoucair/Thames and Hudson
Ltd. 52, 53: (top) John G. Ross, Rome; (bottom) Kodansha
Ltd. 54, 55: MMA. 56, 57: Ernst A. Heiniger, Zurich. 58,
59: MMA. 60, 61: Brooklyn Museum. 62: Seth Joel, N.Y.
63-65: MMA. 66: Jürgen Liepe/ÄM. 68: Skira S.A. 69:
ÄM. 70, 71: EPA/Scala. 72: (left) Maurice Babey/Ziolo;
(center) Dieter Johannes, Munich; (right) Jürgen Liepe/

ÄM. 73: Roger Wood, London. 74: MMA. 75: (left) Uni-
Dia-Verlag, Munich; (right) MMA. 76: John G. Ross,
Rome. 77: Louvre, Paris. 78: Jürgen Liepe/ÄM. 79:
Gulbenkian Museum, University of Durham. 80: Mar-
garete Büsing/ÄM. 81: Timothy Kendall/Museum of Fine
Arts, Boston. 82-85: Norbert Schimmel, N.Y. 86: (top)
Brooklyn Museum; (bottom) Norbert Schimmel, N.Y. 87:
(bottom) Louvre, Paris. 88, 89: Brooklyn Museum. 90, 91:
Norbert Schimmel, N.Y. 92, 93: John G. Ross, Rome. 94,
95: Ashmolean Museum, Oxford. 97: Werner Forman Ar-
chive. 98, 99: John G. Ross, Rome. 100-103: MMA. 104:
John G. Ross, Rome. 105: Lee Boltin, Croton-on-Hudson,
N.Y. 106-117: Kodansha Ltd. 118, 119: Lee Boltin, Croton-
on-Hudson, N.Y. 120: Johann Willsberger, Munich. 121:
Giraudon. 122, 123: Peter Clayton, London. 124, 125: John
G. Ross, Rome. 126-131: Lee Boltin, Croton-on-Hudson,
N.Y. 132, 133: Giraudon. 134-136: Lee Boltin, Croton-on-
Hudson, N.Y. 137: Werner Forman Archive. 138, 139: Lee
Boltin, Croton-on-Hudson, N.Y. 141: George Holton/
Photo Researchers. 142: Vatican, Rome. 143: René Roland/
Ziolo. 144, 145: Brian Brake/Time Inc. 146: Ekkehart Rit-
ter/Akademische Druck- u. Verlagsanstalt, Graz. 147:
Brian Brake/Photo Researchers. 148, 149: Giraudon. 150,
151: Ekkehart Ritter/Akademische Druck- u. Verlagsanstalt, Graz. 152, 153: Oriental Institute, University of Chicago. 154: John G. Ross, Rome. 155: Farrell Grehan/FPG.
156, 157: Giraudon. 158: Giuseppe di Pietro/Mario Ger-
ardi. 159: Farrell Grehan/Photo Researchers. 160, 161: Farrell Grehan/FPG. 162, 163: Claus Hansmann, Stockdorf.
164, 165: Brian Brake/Photo Researchers. 166, 167: Claus
Hansmann, Stockdorf. 168, 169: John G. Ross, Rome.

SUGGESTED READINGS

Aldred, Cyril, *Akhenaten and Nefertiti*. Thames and Hudson Ltd., 1973.

———, *Egyptian Art*. Oxford University Press, 1980.

———, *Jewels of the Pharaohs*. Thames and Hudson Ltd., 1971.

Casson, Lionel, *Daily Life in Ancient Egypt*. American Heritage Publishing Co., 1975.

David, A. Rosalie, *The Egyptian Kingdoms*. Phaidon Press Ltd., 1975.

Desroches-Noblecourt, Christiane, *Tutankhamen*. George Rainbird Ltd., 1963.

Edwards, I.E.S., *Tutankhamun: His Tomb and Its Treasures*. Victor Gollancz Ltd., 1979.

Fakhry, Ahmed, *The Pyramids*. University of Chicago Press, 1961.

Gardiner, Alan, *Egypt of the Pharaohs*. Oxford University Press, 1961.

Hawkes, Jacquetta, *Pharaohs of Egypt*. American Heritage Publishing Co., 1965.

Jenkins, Nancy, *The Boat Beneath the Pyramid*. Holt, Rinehart and Winston, 1980.

Kamel El Mallakh and Arnold C. Brackman, *The Gold of Tutankhamen*. Newsweek Books, 1978.

Mekhitarian, Arpag, *Egyptian Painting*. Rizzoli International Publications, Inc., 1978.

Mertz, Barbara, *Red Land, Black Land*. Dodd, Mead & Co., 1966.

———, *Temples, Tombs and Hieroglyphs*. Dodd, Mead & Co., 1964.

Michalowski, Kazimierz, *Art of Ancient Egypt*. Harry N. Abrams, Inc. 1968.

Montet, Pierre, *Everyday Life in Egypt*. University of Pennsylvania Press, 1981.

Posener, Georges, *A Dictionary of Egyptian Civilization*. Methuen and Co., Ltd., 1962.

Simpson, William Kelly ed., *The Literature of Ancient Egypt*. Yale University Press, 1972.

Smith, William Stevenson, *The Art and Architecture of Ancient Egypt*. Penguin Books, 1958.

Steindorff, George and Keith C. Seele, *When Egypt Ruled the East*. University of Chicago Press, 1957.

Stewart, Desmond, *The Pyramids and Sphinx*. Newsweek Books, 1979.

Wilson, John A., *The Culture of Ancient Egypt*. University of Chicago Press, 1951.

INDEX

Page numbers in **boldface type** refer to illustrations and captions.

A

Abu Simbel (temple), 142, 145, **155-169**
afterlife, beliefs in, **144**
agriculture, 12
  of modern Egypt, 154
Ahhotep (queen, Egypt), **50-53**
Ahmose (pharaoh), 42, **51-53**
  tomb of, **49**
Akhenaten (Amenhotep IV; pharaoh), 67-71, **67, 68,** 80, 140
  Amarna built under, **81-95**
  art under, 71-79, 104
  Book of the Dead proscribed under, **144**
  Nefertiti and, **72-77**
  Smenkhare and, **80**
  Tutankhamen and, 98-101
Akhetaten (Amarna; Egypt), 68, 70-71
  art of, 71-80, **72-77, 81-95,** 104, **124**
Akkadians, 14
alabaster, **129**
Alexander the Great (Alexander III; king, Macedon), 13, 153
Alexandria (Egypt), 153

Amarna (Akhetaten; Egypt), **68,** 70-71
  art of, 71-80, **72-77, 81-95,** 104, **124**
Amen (deity), 44, 67, 69-71, 99, **164-167**
Amenemhet (name of three pharaohs), 21
Amenemhet II (pharaoh), 24
Amenhotep II (pharaoh), 142, 143
Amenhotep III (pharaoh), **40,** 48, **58, 61, 63**
  Akhenaten and, 67
  Tushratta and, 96-98
Amenhotep IV, *see* Akhenaten
Amor (Syria), 152
Anatolia (Turkey), 24
Ankhesenamen (Ankhesenpaaten; queen, Egypt), **97,** 98, 99, 101-102, **124**
Anubis (deity), **144-145, 149**
Apiru (Hebrews), 143
Arabs, 154

Armenia, 24
art
  of Amarna, 71-80, **72-77, 81-95**
  of New Kingdom gold, **100-101**
  of Tutankhamen's tomb, 104, **105-139**
Assyrians, 153
astronomy, Great Pyramid and, **16**
Aswan (Syene; Egypt), 13
Aten (deity), 69-71, **84, 86,** 99
  House of, **83**
Ay (pharaoh), **69, 70,** 99

B

Baghdad (Iraq), 154
beds, **22-23**
boats
  in tomb of Cheops, **18**
  in tomb of Tutankhamen, **129**
Book of the Dead, **144, 147, 150**
Britain, 154
bulls, **152**
burials, 15-20
  see also pyramids; tombs

C

Canaan, 143
Canaanites, 14
canals, 12
Carnarvon, Lord, 103-104
carnelian (gem), 22, **50**
 in tombs of daughters of Senusret II,
  27, 31, 38
 in tomb of Tutankhamen, **133**
Carter, Howard, 103-104
Chefren (Khafre; pharaoh), 13-14
Cheops (Khufu; pharaoh), Great
  Pyramid of, 13-15, **16-19**
clergy
 Akhenaten and, 71
 Tutankhamen and, 99
climate, 11
cloisonné, **27, 32, 126-127**
commerce
 under Hatshepsut, 43, **44-45**
 of Middle Kingdom, 22, 24
Constantinople (Turkey), 154
cosmetics, **36**
cotton, 154

D

Daggers, **52-53, 126-127**
Dahshur (Egypt), 22
Damascus (Syria), 154
diadems, **122**
Djehutyhotep (prince, Egypt), **24**
Djoser (pharaoh), **11**, 13
dynasties
 First, 13
 Fourth, 14
 Seventeenth, 41
 Eighteenth, 42-48, **51-65**, 67-80,
  96-104
 Nineteenth, 140-152, **154**
 Thirty-first, 13

E

Egypt
 under Akhenaten, 67-80
 Amarna as capital of, **81-95**
 under Eighteenth Dynasty, 42-48,
  51-65
 gold art of, **100-101**
 under Greek rule, 153-154
 under Hatshepsut, **45**
 under Hyksos, 41-42
 map of, **8**
 under Menes, 12-13
 under Middle Kingdom, 21-24
 under Old Kingdom, 20-21
 under Ramses II, 140-152
 Ramses II's buildings in, **155-169**
 under Tutankhamen, 96-104
 Tutankhamen's tomb and, **105-139**
Eighteenth Dynasty, 42-48, **51-65**
 Akhenaten and, 67-80
 Jews during, 142-143
 Tutankhamen and, 96-104, **105-139**
Ethiopia, 44, 96
Exodus, 142-145, 152

F

Fayum (desert, Egypt), 21
First Dynasty, 13
forced labor, 142
Fourth Dynasty, 14
furniture, **22-23, 51**

G

Gemstones, 22-24, **50**
 in Eighteenth Dynasty, 47
 in tombs of daughters of Senusret II,
  27, 31
 in tomb of Tutankhamen, **118-121,
  124, 126-127, 133, 134**
Giza (Egypt), Great Pyramids of, 13-14,
  16-19
glass, **100**
 in tomb of Tutankhamen, **113,
  120-121, 124, 137**

H

gold, 11
 in Eighteenth Dynasty, 47-48, **51,
  55, 57, 70**
 jewelry of, 22
 of New Kingdom, **100-101**
 from Nubia, 21
 of Ptolemies, 154
 in tomb of Ahhotep, **50**
 in tombs of daughters of Senusret II,
  27, 31, 32, 34, 38
 in tomb of Tutankhamen, 96-98,
  **107, 109, 113, 118-122, 124,
  126-127, 129, 131, 133, 134,
  137**
government
 corruption in, 48
 under Eighteenth Dynasty, 44
 under Old Kingdom, 14-15
Great Britain, 154
Great Pyramid (of Khufu; Cheops; in
  Giza), 13-15, **16-19**
Great Sphinx (Giza), 14
Great Temple (Abu Simbel), **157**
Great Temple (Karnak), **166-167**
Greece, 153-154

H

Habiru (Hebrews), 143
Haremhab (pharaoh), 99-101, 140
Hatshepsut (pharaoh), 42-43, **44-45**
Hebrews, 143-145
Herodotus, 12, 14, 96
Hetepheres (queen, Egypt), **22-23**
Hittites, 101-102, 145
Horus (deity), **25, 31, 143**
House of Aten (Amarna), **83**
hunting, 101
Huy, **102**
Hyksos, 24, 41-42, **52-53**

I

Isis (deity), **109**
Islam, 154
ivory, **129, 131**

Jewelry
  of Eighteenth Dynasty, 47-48, **51, 57**
  of New Kingdom, **50**
  in tombs of daughters of Senusret II,
    22, **25-39**
Jews, 142-145
Joseph, 142-143

Kamose, 41, **51**
Karnak (Egypt), 69, 99
  Ramses II's buildings at, 142, 145,
    157, 164-167
  see also Thebes
Kha-em-opet, 48
Khafre (Chefren; pharaoh), 13-14
Khnumet (princess, Egypt), **27, 31, 32**
Khufu (Cheops; pharaoh), Great
  Pyramid of, 13-15, **16-19**

Lapis lazuli (gem), 22-24
  of Eighteenth Dynasty, 47, **51, 57**
  in tomb of Ahhotep, **50**
  in tombs of daughters of Senusret
    II, **27, 31, 38**
  in tomb of Tutankhamen, **118-119,
    133, 134**
Lebanon, 43, 44
life expectancy, 20
Lower Egypt, **8,** 152
Luxor (Egypt)
  Ramses II's buildings at, **157**
  see also Thebes

Maat (deity), **109**
Manetho, 13
Mecca (Saudi Arabia), 154
Menes (first pharaoh), 12-13
Menhet, **54**
Menkaure (Mycerinus; pharaoh), 13-14
Menwi, **54**
Mereret (princess, Egypt), **27, 28**
Merneptah (pharaoh), 143

Merti, **54**
Merytaten, **80**
Middle Kingdom (2000-1800 B.C.),
    21-24
  jewelry of, **25-39**
Mitanni, 68, 96
monotheism, 71
Morgan, Jacques de, 22
mummification, 15
Mycerinus (Menkaure; pharaoh), 13-14

Nakht, **42, 43,** 48
Neferneferuatentasherit (princess,
    Egypt), **95**
Neferneferure (princess, Egypt), **95**
Nefertari (queen, Egypt), **147-151, 157,
    161**
Nefertiti (queen, Egypt), 67-68, **67,
    72-77,** 79, **86-88,** 98
Nekhbet (deity), **50, 134, 137, 158**
Nephthys (deity), **109**
New Kingdom (1576-1069 B.C.)
  afterlife beliefs in, 144
  gold of, **100-101**
  jewelry of, **50**
Nile River, **8,** 12, 13, 154
  Abu Simbel temple on, **157**
  climate along, 11
  flooding of, 14
Nineteenth Dynasty, 140-152
  amusements of, **154**
  gold of, 21, 96, 154
  Tutankhamen and, **102**
nuby (goldsmith), **100**

Oil, 154
Old Kingdom (2700-2200 B.C.), 13-21
  silver in tombs of, 24
Osiris (deity)
  in afterlife beliefs, **144**

portrayed at Abu Simbel, **158**
portrayed in tomb of Nefertari,
    149, 150
portrayed in tomb of Tutankhamen,
    109, 113, 120-121
"Ozymandias" (poem, Shelley), 142

Palestine, 43, 44, **51,** 140, 145
  Jews in, 143
papyrus, **14,** 143
Pepi II (pharaoh), 20-21
Persians, 153
Petrie, Sir Flinders, 22, 103
petroleum, 154
pharaohs, 14-15
  of Greek descent, 153
  see also individual pharaohs
Pi-Rameses (Raamses; Tanis; Egypt),
    143-145, 152
Pithom (Egypt), 143
Ptolemy I (Ptolemy Soter; pharaoh),
    153, 154
Ptolemy II (pharaoh), 154
Punt (Sudan), 43, **44-45**
pyramids
  Cheops' (Great), 14, 15, **16-19**
  Djoser's, **11,** 13
  map of, **8**
  of Middle Kingdom, 22
  see also tombs

Raamses (Pi-Rameses; Tanis; Egypt),
    143-145, 152
Ramesseum (Karnak), 142
Ramose, 70, 79
Ramses I (pharaoh), 140, 143
Ramses II (User-maat-re; pharaoh),
    140-152, **141, 143, 152**
  Book of the Dead used under, **144**
  buildings built by, **155-169**
  Nefertari and, **147-151**
Ramses III (pharaoh), 152
Ramses IV (pharaoh), 103
Re (deity), 69, **120-121, 137, 143**

Re-Harakhti (deity), **109, 157**
religion
    afterlife in, **144**
    of Akhenaten, 68-71
    during decline of Egypt, 153
    deities in, 15
    during Eighteenth Dynasty, 44
    pharaohs in, 14
    of Tutankhamen, 99
Rome, 154

Sakkara (Egypt), **12, 14**
scarabs, **63**
    in tomb of Tutankhamen, **133, 137**
senet (game), **61**
Senusret (name of three pharaohs), 21
Senusret II (pharaoh), 22
    tombs of daughters of, **25-39**
Senusret III (pharaoh), 22, 24, **27**
Seti I (pharaoh), 140, **164**
Seventeenth Dynasty, 41
shen, **50**
ships
    in tomb of Cheops, **18**
    in tomb of Tutankhamen, **129**
Shu (deity), **131**
silver, 24
    of Eighteenth Dynasty, **51, 54**
Sit-Hathor-Yunet (princess, Egypt), 22,
    27, 32, 34, 36, 38
slavery, 14, **78**
    of Jews, 142-143
Smenkhare (pharaoh), 79-80, **80**
Snefru (pharoah), **23**
Sphinx (Giza), 14
sphinxes, **50, 166-167**
Sudan, **51**, 153
Sumerians, 14
swords, **52-53**
Syene (Aswan; Egypt), 13
Syria, **51**

Tanis (Raamses; Pi-Rameses; Egypt),
    143-145, 152
temples
    in Amarna, **81, 83**
    to Amen, 44-46
    to Aten, 69, 70
    built under Ramses II, 142, 145, **152,**
        155-169
    to Hatshepsut, 43, **44-45**
    to Tiy, **68**
Thebes (Egypt)
    as capital, 44-48, **51**
    capital moved to Amarna from, 70,
        71
    capital moved to Raamses from, 145
    capital returned to, 80, 99
    under Hyksos, 24
    Ramses II's buildings at, **157,**
        162-163
    temple to Hatshepsut in, **44-45**
    tombs at, **46**, 152
    Valley of the Queens in, **147**
    see also Karnak
Thirty-first Dynasty, 13
Thoth (deity), **137, 150**
Thutmose I (pharaoh), 42, 46
Thutmose II (pharaoh), 42
Thutmose III (pharaoh), 42-44, **45, 54,**
    57, 142
    Jews under, 143
Ti (Old Kingdom dignitary), **12**
Ti (wife of Ay), 70
Tiy (queen, Egypt), 48, **58, 65**, 68, **75**
tombs, **15**, 20, **20, 21**
    afterlife and, **144**
    Ahhotep's, **50-53**
    Ahmose's, **49**
    near Amarna, 80
    artisans portrayed in, **100**
    Cheops', 15
    of daughters of Senusret II, 22, **25-39**
    during decline of Egypt, 153
    Djehutyhoteps', **24**
    of Eighteenth Dynasty, 46-47, **46, 51**
    Hetepheres', **22-23**
    Huy's, **102**
    of Middle Kingdom, 22

    Nakht's, **42, 43, 48**
    Nefertari's, **147-151**
    Ramose's, 69-70, 79
    Ramses II's, 152
    robberies of, 21, 47-48
    at Sakkara, **12, 14**
    silver in, 24
    Tutankhamen's, 98, 102-104, **105-139**
    of wives of Thutmose III, **57**
    see also pyramids
trade, *see* commerce
Turks, 154
turquoise (gem), 22-24, 47, **50**
    in tombs of daughters of Senusret II,
        27, 31
Tushratta (king of Mitanni), 96-98
Tutankhamen (Tutankhaten; pharaoh),
    80, 96-102, **97, 98, 102**, 140
    gold of, **100**
    tomb of, 102-104, **105-139**
Tuy (queen, Egypt), **142**

Upper Egypt, **8**, 152
User-maat-re, *see* Ramses II

Valley of the Kings (Egypt), 46, 103
    Tutankhamen's tomb in, **107**
Valley of the Queens (Thebes), **147**

Wars
    between Greece and Egypt, 153
    Hebrews taken captive in, 143
    between Hittites and Egypt, 145
    between Hyksos and Egypt, 24, 41-42
    of Old Kingdom, 20
weapons, **52-53**
wine, 42